WHEN THE GARDEN ISN'T EDEN

WHEN THE GARDEN ISN'T EDEN

MORE PSYCHODYNAMIC CONCEPTS FROM LIFE

KERRY L. MALAWISTA, LINDA G. KANEFIELD, AND ANNE J. ADELMAN

Columbia University Press
New York

Columbia University Press
Publishers Since 1893
New York   Chichester, West Sussex
cup.columbia.edu
Copyright © 2022 Columbia University Press

Library of Congress Cataloging-in-Publication Data
Names: Malawista, Kerry L., author. | Kanefield, Linda, author. | Adelman,
    Anne J., author.
Title: When the garden isn't Eden : more psychodynamic concepts from life /
    Kerry L. Malawista, Linda Kanefield, and Anne J. Adelman.
Description: New York : Columbia University Press, [2022] | Includes
    bibliographical references and index.
Identifiers: LCCN 2021054733 (print) | LCCN 2021054734 (ebook) |
    ISBN 9780231170369 (hardback) | ISBN 9780231170376
    (trade paperback) | ISBN 9780231555753 (ebook)
Subjects: LCSH: Storytelling—Psychological aspects. | Psychology—
    Biographical methods. | Discourse analysis, Narrative—Psychological
    aspects. | Self-perception.
Classification: LCC BF39.4 .M35 2022 (print) | LCC BF39.4 (ebook) |
    DDC 155.2—dc23/eng/20211220
LC record available at https://lccn.loc.gov/2021054733
LC ebook record available at https://lccn.loc.gov/2021054734

Cover design: Julia Kushnirsky
Cover illustration: Gracia Lam

KLM: To Robert Winer and Sharon Alperovitz, for creating *New Directions in Writing*.

LGK: To my tenth-grade English teacher, Mrs. Virginia Clater, who taught me how to think about what I read and how to write about what I think.

AJA: To the memory of my parents' store, Osner Typewriters and Business Machines, where I learned as a child to peck out my first stories on a Royal Deluxe portable.

CONTENTS

Part Two: Development

Part Three: Therapeutic Listening

Part Four: Transitions and Challenges

WHEN THE GARDEN ISN'T EDEN

INTRODUCTION

Kerry L. Malawista

When we lose the stories we have believed about ourselves, we are losing more than stories, we are losing ourselves.

—Lauren Goff, *Arcadia*

In 2017, six years after the publication of *Wearing My Tutu to Analysis and Other Stories*, my husband and I attended a conference on Psychoanalysis and the Arts in Florence, Italy. One afternoon, while strolling down one of those quiet medieval streets, a woman scurried past, paused to check her map, and then abruptly backtracked along the same cobblestone path we were on.

As she approached, I noticed she was wearing a badge from the same conference. Giving a wave of my badge, I invited her to walk with us, since we were going to the same lecture.

Walking side by side, I introduced myself.

"Oh, the *Tutu* author!" she squealed in English with a French lilt. "I love the *Tutu* book. I use it when I teach candidates back in Paris. The stories are the perfect way to teach. I hope you'll write another."

Now it was my turn to squeal. It was as if this stranger had told me that she knew my children and elaborated on their talents. I was delighted that someone from as far away as France appreciated our premise that psychotherapy and stories form a perfect union.[1] In the introduction to that first book, I wrote about the importance of stories, how they fire the imagination and are a powerful way to teach complicated ideas. Stories, even simple ones, can capture a deeper wisdom about human nature that can resonate long after they're heard.

When the Garden Isn't Eden, our follow-up to the "*Tutu* book," brings a new set of psychological concepts to life through stories, both personal and clinical. Although our colleague and friend Catherine Anderson could not join us this time, we are fortunate to have the wonderful collaboration of Linda Kanefield.

In this volume, the three of us offer vignettes and reflections that illuminate how therapists think and work. Each chapter can be understood in light of important psychodynamic concepts and ideas that reflect the authenticity of our voices but not the full range of our own and others' experiences. We hope that the material conveys a universality that readers can relate to and embrace.

We believe that psychoanalysis, especially in the midst of evolving sociopolitical unrest, continues to offer a unique window into the complexity of the human mind. It provides a language to describe the unconscious motivations that underlie our actions, perceptions, and relationships with ourselves and others. As psychoanalysts, we fiercely embrace the calls for change and accept the challenge to break through historical complacency. We hope to emerge with a sharpened vision and a more finely tuned insight into those on the margins— and into what has kept them there. It is our hope that the stories in *When the Garden Isn't Eden* invite the reader to reflect on these issues and to understand what psychoanalysis brings to bear on our humanity.

Our sense of self, our hopes and fears, and what we anticipate in our relationships shape the stories of who we are. It is the accumulation of these life stories—our narrative memories—that casts a shadow on our current lives, bringing forth new versions of old feelings and conflicts. Who we are in the present is continually influenced by what we remember from the past, as well as what we don't remember. This idea is introduced in our opening story, "When the Garden Isn't Eden," which explores how a traumatic experience—embedded in the body and inaccessible to conscious awareness or language—can continue to influence us in unexpected ways.

While we may think of memories as a reenactment of what "really" happened—as facts—they are instead "personal truths," recollections that are continually added to and subtracted from each time they are remembered. In fact, we can never fully recapture what we experienced at a particular time in the past. It is impossible to be an accurate witness to our own life. Unwittingly, we commit time-slice errors, adding details from other times, or we confabulate time periods, moving a memory to an earlier time, one where it better fits the narrative we have created. Hence, memories are more imagined than remembered. As the neurologist and essayist Oliver Sacks (2013) tells us, our only truth is narrative truth.

With narrative truth we continually reinterpret, reorganize, and retell our stories to keep pace with our current emotional state or to align with what we believe to be true at that moment. It is this plasticity of memory, the ability to rework painful memories in a constructive way, that is essential to resilience and offers the possibility of changing our future. A shared narrative, especially of trauma, helps us heal.

Those suffering from traumatic life events and destructive relationships tend to hold fossilized memories—rigid, unchanging stories of sad and painful events. While they are of course "true" stories, these narratives are not easily revised. Although they are anchored in the past, they offer no acceptance of the present and preclude the sense of self and agency necessary to meet the future. Instead, these hard-shelled memories form a fixed life story, one without the gaps and flexibility to morph and shift, so that their present and future become equally stuck and fossilized.

Psychodynamic treatment provides a setting to search for and ferret out these "truths," or long-held beliefs, finding patterns and connections. In therapy, we begin to understand why certain stories are held on to while others slip away. Through the questioning and introspection of the bits and pieces of one's remembered past—in the context of a secure relationship—we begin to create new and healthier self-narratives. The story can then shift from one that may only say, "This was horrific. There is no more to say," to a richer and more nuanced narrative.

Herein lies the transformative quality of treatment—the opportunity to seek a literal *re*-vision, a new way of seeing what has happened in one's life. This does not mean the past literally changes or that the new version ends with "we lived happily ever after." While neuroscientists tell us that the simple act of recalling memories changes the brain's organic structure, they are not referring to the reciting of memory alone. The brain is altered through the process of reexamining the painful remembered narratives in the present, which allows us to see how they continue to influence our current lives and relationships in self-defeating ways. Our reworking of the past allows us to create a future different from the one we had imagined or expected when we were constrained by our earlier locked-in narrative. As resilience develops, we see that our patients no longer relate their memories as fixed, glued in place by familiar painful affect. We move forward together, co-creating a new and richer narrative that leads to growth and a more flexible way of seeing oneself in the world.

We have divided this book into four main sections: "Clinical Thoughts," "Development," "Therapeutic Listening," and "Transitions and Challenges." Neither the scope of the sections nor the range of topics addressed within each is intended to provide a comprehensive overview of psychodynamic thought. Rather, these vignettes create a window through which to view the complex and compelling world of psychodynamic thinking. Once the readers' appetites have been whetted by these stories, we hope they will be inspired to continue their exploration through further study.

Part 1, "Clinical Thoughts," is an introduction to the fundamental concepts we did not address in our first book, including somatic memory, projective identification, mentalization, the uncanny, and identification. Of course, a story is never about one thing, so these vignettes allow us to circle back to concepts and ideas that we shared in our first book, such as *transference*, *enactment*, and *magical thinking*. Like a quilt, each story adds another square that deepens our understanding of how the unconscious mind works.

Part 2, "Development," comprises five vignettes of common developmental experiences—separation anxiety and sibling rivalry, two stories that explore painful and traumatic events that can derail development, and old age and its effects on adult children.

Part 3, "Therapeutic Listening," explores the clinical space, which informs the reader about how a psychotherapist listens to and engages with patients—the empathy, attunement, timing, tact, reverie, and working-through that contribute to the success or disruption of a treatment. The final chapter in this section explores self-disclosure. Together, these stories reveal the powerful processes at work in our sessions with patients.

Part 4, "Transitions and Challenges," deals with the changes, losses, and events that we all experience in life, both as therapists and patients. We share three narratives that include frozen grief, an adolescent's experience of an adult male's sexual violation, and resilience. The final two chapters address our current national crises: COVID-19 showed up and changed the way we treat patients, friends, beloved customs, and milestones; at the same time, our nation has begun to collectively face our long history of racism.

When the Garden Isn't Eden brings together storytelling and psychotherapy. We invite all of you to join us, as students, clinicians, and curious readers, to view the fascinating and complex world of development and human experience through a psychodynamic lens. Our narratives vary widely in detail, yet the themes are familiar: we love, we hate, we yearn, we fear, we grieve for what we've lost, and we celebrate what is to come.

PART ONE
Clinical Thoughts

I WHEN THE GARDEN ISN'T EDEN

My husband and I went with friends to see *When the Garden Was Eden*, a documentary about the New York Knicks' stunning NBA championship win over the LA Lakers. I was never a basketball fan, so I had only a vague familiarity with two of the star players: Walt Frazier and Bill Bradley. Yet as I watched the film I was captivated by how this "dream team" of black and white players united New York City during a period of racial conflict and political unrest.

The movie audience and I cheered along with the Madison Square Garden fans as we watched the archived footage of the Knicks winning the championship. Then just as the audience erupts in a victorious roar—the Knicks won by fourteen points—I was suddenly struck with what can only be described as a punch to the gut, a sickening jolt of dread. As the crowd continued to applaud, I sat in stunned silence, my heart racing, trying to make sense of this inexplicable heaviness and sadness that had suddenly overtaken me at the moment the Knicks won.

A buzz of excited voices followed us out of the theater. The six of us strolled to a nearby restaurant for dinner, and I lingered behind.

The fog that descended while watching the film still surrounded me. Such overwhelming sadness was rare for me. So where did this come from?

Once seated at the restaurant, after we ordered wine and appetizers, I tried to untangle what had happened to me back in the theater. Interrupting their conversation, I asked my friends, "Do any of you remember what year that was, when the Knicks won the NBA championship?"

One of my friends thought 1969, another guessed 1970 or 1971. Hearing that year—1970—I pulled out my iPhone and search for "Knicks win NBA championship." Up popped the headline "Knicks Win It!" with the date May 8, 1970.

That day—May 8, 1970—is seared in my memory. It is the day after my mother died. I was nine years old.

The image of me standing at our front door and holding the May 8 edition of the *Bergen Record* flashed through my mind. The headline at the top of the paper was no doubt about the Knicks winning, but below the fold was a large photograph of my family's Ford Country Squire station wagon, smashed in, glass shattered. In that moment, the intoxicating smell of the burgundy leather seats also returned. It was our family's first new car. I remembered at the time feeling that I was looking at something I shouldn't be seeing.

Transported back to that morning, I now recall reading the caption below the photograph: "A woman was killed and her small son critically injured in Palisades Park." I didn't want to imagine a "woman," my mother, pressed inside what looked like an enormous accordion with all the air pressed out of it.

At that moment, one of my aunts walked over and gently took the newspaper from me, saying, "You don't want to see that." But I *had* seen it. I had read the caption, and my brain had no doubt parked it along with the banner headline above the fold that day—"Knicks Win It!"

Now in the restaurant looking at my phone, I realized that I must have seen—but not registered—the headline of the Knicks' miraculous win. The movie about that win was the unlikely key to what had been a locked-down memory of my mother's death. It had been decades since I had felt as grief-stricken as I did in that movie theater. Or perhaps it was the first time.

My brain knew the date, but my body still knows the sorrow.

Analysts Reflect on Somatic Memory

The body knows things [of] which the mind is ignorant.

—Jacques LeCoq

Where does a story live when there are no words or images to tell it?

Our author watches the finale of the film *When the Garden Was Eden*, and it sparks a physical sensation—*a punch to the gut, a sickening jolt of dread*—without an accompanying conscious narrative to make sense of it. This moment captures a complex truth of the brain's trickery: emotional memories can remain hidden in the body, inaccessible to conscious awareness.

It is not until the storyteller looks up the date that she realizes that two events—her mother's death and the Knicks' win—are emotionally interwoven, leaving a bodily imprint linked by two headlines. *I had read the caption, and my brain had no doubt parked it along with the banner headline above the fold that day—"Knicks Win It!"* The pain of losing her mother remained embedded in the storyteller's body, but she had no conscious access to the narrative memory of her mother's death.

Latency ushers in a period of rapid cognitive growth that outpaces the child's emotional understanding. At age nine, this young girl has the cognitive capacity to understand that her mother has died in a terrible car accident. However, the powerful fantasy that the loved one is still alive offers psychological protection from unbearable pain and the finality of her loss.

In those first traumatic hours, her young brain was unable to register the overwhelming loss of her mother's death. Her pain cleaved, in a sense, to this emotionally compelling concurrent event: the Knicks' win. The intensity of affect associated with these two events remained latent in her body. Over the course of her development, these facts coalesced unconsciously into a cohesive narrative. As Bessel van der Kolk (1996) writes, "When we are overwhelmed by trauma, the body keeps the score" (214).

Until she watched the movie, the storyteller's full range of affect remained inaccessible, unlinked to memory. There were not yet words for the powerful feelings of inconsolability. These feelings remained hidden from our storyteller's cognitive awareness, but they were preserved in her body. When her grief was awakened at the end of the film, she could not explain the intensity of her reaction. *As the crowd continued to applaud, I sat in stunned silence, my heart racing, trying to make sense of this inexplicable heaviness and sadness that had suddenly overtaken me at the moment the Knicks won.*

Our author has neither a conscious memory of the Knicks winning the NBA championship nor of its concurrent timing with her mother's death. While we can imagine that our narrator likely read the May 8 headline when she picked up the newspaper the morning after her mother died, she is completely blindsided by her intense emotions fifty years later in a movie theater.

This moment gives a glimpse into the way our psyche protects us from painful, retrievable memories. Just as the body naturally mends after a physical injury, the mind, too, has ways of reworking, repairing, and reshaping our traumatic memories. By "outsourcing" an unbearable memory as a somatic, nonverbal one, we are better able to move forward, allow healing, and not be left mired in grief. Yet in the end, just as our body carries the scars of physical injuries, it also carries the traces of our emotional wounds. If an individual cannot form a narrative of traumatic events that weaves together affect and reflection, such events can limit one's emotional or relational life in problematic or unexpected ways. How this unfolds in a particular individual depends on many factors, including one's genetic and constitutional disposition, cultural and family dynamics, and life experiences.

To better understand the way memories are stored, we turn to the work of the Swiss neurologist Édouard Claparède (1911). He demonstrates that traumatic emotions are registered in the soma (body), without a conscious awareness of their existence. He describes a patient who had lost all short-term memory after a brain injury. Every day this woman shook the doctor's hand as if they were meeting for the first time. One day, he hid a tack in his hand. The following day, Claparède greeted his patient, and, as expected, she did not recall ever meeting him. But this time when he offered his hand, she pulled back and refused to shake it. When asked why she would not shake his hand, she could offer no explanation, but she knew instinctively to avoid it.

The body and its instincts, as well as the mind and memory, contain one's life story.

In the seventh and final volume of *In Search of Lost Time*, *Time Regained*, Marcel Proust captures the reawakening of his affective memories when he strolls along the uneven streets of Paris (1981, 7:255). Proust speaks to the power of affective memory being stirred by a sensory trigger—a familiar smell, touch, sight, or sound. In our storyteller's case, her acute bodily reaction was triggered by a movie.

The evocative cue—hearing the Knicks win—triggers the amygdala, the brain's emotional center. Even though the memory of viewing the newspaper article remained forgotten or was never encoded verbally, her body remembered what the mind had not processed. As an adult, she could now integrate the enormous pain and grief she had pushed away as a nine-year-old child. The intense affect that broke through while watching the film allowed her to form a new narrative memory of her mother's death, one that holds both emotion and remembrance.

While it is generally understood that the frontal lobe and amygdala contribute to the creation of memories, these structures reveal nothing of the phenomenology of how we feel when we recall our cherished memories—our child's kiss at bedtime, our dog's greeting each morning, or how it feels to lose a loved one. We can compare the difference between our knowledge of neuroanatomy and our understanding of a richly textured memory to the difference between reading a recipe for pasta puttanesca and tasting the full-of-flavor dish.

Jeffrey Eugenides writes in *Middlesex*, "Biology gives you a brain. Life turns it into a mind."

When the body remembers, it's as if the trauma is happening right now. Time collapses, and there is no sense of the past. All the powerful unprocessed grief of that long-ago moment is reexperienced in raw form. What our storyteller experienced in the movie theater and then examined at length offered her the opportunity to link her emotional memory to her recalled experience. By integrating it more fully and encoding it more cohesively in her narrative memory, she is better able to heal from a profound loss.

Perhaps for all of us, the body is where our deepest sorrows lie.

2 A VISITATION

I awoke unsettled, weary from a night of disturbing dreams, all of them about Kimmy. In one of them, she was running through an open, lush field, frantically searching. When she sees me, she darts over and begins pulling at my arm, signaling for me to join her, but I don't know how to help her. In another, she is sitting in a chair weeping, her dark wavy hair falling across her face, while I stand nearby, helpless to comfort her—that is the one that roused me.

Over breakfast and still groggy, I tell my husband about my dreams and how they felt more like a visitation. While he had never met Kimmy, he knows her well through my stories of growing up. For me, she conjures up the feeling of a childhood blankie, well loved and always at hand.

I was almost five when I saw the moving van pull up to the house across the street, and I hoped that a girl was moving in. Among the boxes being unloaded from the truck, a fancy dollhouse and a kitchen set caught my eye. Soon after, a girl who looked about my age climbed out of the car that had pulled in behind the van.

I crossed the street and asked her name. Kimmy. My sisters and I all had names beginning with a "K" sound. She told me how she and her mother were moving in but that her father had stayed behind.

For the next four years—a lifetime in childhood—Kimmy and I were inseparable. We spoke in "Spanish" to each other. It was really just gibberish, but we were certain everyone thought we were from some faraway country.

My father often said, "You two are like twins." Yet no one could have taken us for real twins: she was Italian, with dark brown eyes and hair, and she still had a bit of baby fat, while I was tall and scrawny, with light green eyes and sandy brown hair.

Most days, I'd dash across the street to play with her, and there she would be, at the exact same moment, running across to find me. But Kimmy, an only child, always preferred my house, because I had three sisters. There we would set up elaborate games of house or school, always arguing over whose turn it was to be the mother or the teacher. Other days we'd play board games; early on it was Chutes and Ladders and Candy Land, and then when we were older, hours and hours of Monopoly or Sorry.

Like sisters, Kimmy and I fought as intensely as we loved. Board games were a battle to the end. For me, some of the frenzy of competition was my jealousy that Kimmy had everything I didn't have (but wanted). She had her own bedroom—the one I had dreamed of—with a canopy bed covered in white netting, fancy white sheets, and ruffled pillows. Her shelves were filled with beautiful dolls perfectly presented. My dolls had their hair chopped off, were missing limbs, or had one eye open and one shut. Kimmy envied me my sisters.

When I was nine, Kimmy's mother and father reunited, and she moved twenty miles away. I recall sitting on the curb outside her house, imagining that, somehow, if I sat there long enough, she might magically return. We saw each other from time to time, but gradually our lives took us in different directions.

Now here it was forty years later, and Kimmy was once again in the forefront of my mind.

After finishing my coffee, I head off to the office. While I often remember my dreams, sometimes vividly, usually the impact fades. Yet these visions of a frantic, grief-stricken Kimmy haunt me all day with a persistence I can't escape or understand.

Arriving home from work, I sit with my husband and say to him, "It's the strangest thing. I feel like something terrible has happened to Kimmy. It makes no sense."

I grab my laptop and bring it to the kitchen table. "I'm going to look her up. Find out what's happening in her life," I say. Searching her name, I find a long-ago wedding announcement. Next I search for "Kimberly" alongside what I think might be her married name. There, in the first entry, is the headline "Teen Killed in Crash." My stomach clenches as I click on the link. The teen in the article is Kimmy's eighteen-year-old son. He died the previous night in a car accident, at the same time that I was dreaming about Kimmy.

I pick up the phone and call her.

Analysts Reflect on the Uncanny

> The most beautiful experience we can have is the mysterious.
>
> —Albert Einstein

As Einstein understood, there are encounters or events in our lives that are outside our undertanding of science, of space and time—even outside what we can perceive with our five senses. This chapter's vignette captures such an incident. The author wakes from disturbing dreams of her childhood friend Kimmy in great distress and grief. The next day, haunted by these images, she decides to search for her friendon the internet and learns that her dreams have coincided with the death of Kimmy's eighteen-year-old son. Psychoanalysts have come to refer to experiences such as these as *the uncanny*.

The *Oxford English Dictionary* defines the uncanny as an occurrence that is strange, mysterious, or unsettling. "Canny" is from the

Anglo-Saxon root "*ken*," which means a comprehensible, knowable, mental perception. The term "uncanny" was first used in 1906 by the German psychiatrist Ernst Jentsch, in his essay "On the Psychology of the Uncanny" (1906), to describe something that is new and unknown and initially seen as negative. He wrote that "someone to whom something 'uncanny' happens is not quite 'at home' or 'at ease' in the situation concerned, that the thing is or at least seems to be foreign to him."

When Freud first introduced the world to the radical notions of the unconscious, the significance of dreams, and the talking cure, he was venturing into the sphere of the uncanny. What an enormous leap to grasp that talking about one's innermost thoughts could lead to psychological change and symptom relief!

In 1919, Sigmund Freud shifted the meaning of the uncanny: not only did it signify something that was not just beyond one's knowledge or perception, but, crucially, it was also both frightening *and* familiar. For example, when we see a ventriloquist's doll or a clown that appears to come to life, or when it seems like a thought we have had made something happen in the world, we venture into the territory of the uncanny. In these complex moments, the line between the real and unreal, between the frightening and the familiar, is blurry.

We probably all have had an uncanny experience. For example, just when we pick up the phone to call a friend, that same friend calls us. Or we may dream about an event, and then something oddly similar is reported on TV. The former we would probably explain as coincidence; in the latter, we might assume that we had overheard something of that event on the news or from some other source without any conscious recall of having heard it.

The uncanny is common in the experience of déjà vu, where we have a vague memory of something we cannot fully recall. Marcel Proust famously wrote of such an experience in his novel *In Search of Lost Time*:

I had just seen, standing a little way back from the hog's-back road along which we were travelling, three trees which probably marked the entry to a covered driveway and formed a pattern which I was not seeing for the first time. I could not succeed in reconstructing the place from which they had been as it were detached, but I felt that it had been familiar to me once; so that, my mind having wavered between some distant year and the present moment. . . . [The] surroundings began to dissolve and I wondered whether the whole of the drive were not a make-believe.

(1981, 2:404)

Most theorists believe that in déjà vu moments such as Proust's, we are picking up cues in a current environment that resemble those in an old one.

Was the uncanny dream about Kimmy just a particularly startling coincidence, one that can be explained by the laws of statistics? Yes, maybe even likely. Could she have somehow heard of her friend's loss beforehand? No. There was no chance the narrator had heard this tragic news. The death occurred in the middle of the night, and the author, living three hundred miles away from her childhood friend, had had no contact with her or anyone in her family for decades. Yet, despite this time and distance, this particular childhood bond remained a psychically powerful one. She speaks of Kimmy as one might describe a transitional object: she *conjured up the feeling of a childhood blankie, well loved and always at hand*. And like a transitional object, Kimmy had faded into the past. Interestingly, Freud ([1919] 1955) wrote that uncanny experiences often lead "back to something long known to us, once very familiar" (219).

Or, we may wonder, does this narrative open the door to the possibility that there are certain experiences and relationships that allow us to *know* something in ways that cannot be explained by what we know about our minds, our theories of physics and neuroscience, and our comprehension of the world?

Early in his career, Freud was fascinated with just such occult phenomena and shared this interest with his close friend and colleague Carl Jung. Jung, a strong believer in the paranormal, would later be known for his writings on the collective unconscious and synchronicity. Jung defined synchronicity as meaningful coincidences, where two events happen at the same time with no causal relationship.

Unlike Jung, Freud feared that psychoanalysis would be rejected as unscientific if psychoanalysts spoke openly about or published their ideas on parapsychology and paranormal phenomena. Instead, Freud's writings emphasize that humans turn to the supernatural as a defense against feelings of overwhelming helplessness, by reconnecting with the omnipotence of an all-knowing being. He asserted that the uncanny experience springs from our hidden impulses, arising from the residues of the earliest stages of development, when the infant has the experience of being omnipotent in thought through his or her merger with a powerful caretaker. In this way the uncanny event signifies the return of a previously repressed, forgotten event. Its reappearance derives from the compulsion to repeat in an effort to master an experience that was previously unintegrated.

Freud further linked fears of the unexplained to the psychological need for and creation of religion. He was steadfast in his efforts to establish psychoanalysis as a science (versus a religion), but Freud scholars highlight the extent to which psychoanalysis was heavily influenced by Freud's Judaism (Richards 2014). In Freud's view, an individual with good reality testing, whose mind was clearly differentiated from external reality and other minds, would not be prone to uncanny experiences. Nevertheless, fourteen years after writing "The Uncanny," Freud wrote in "Dreams and Occultism" (1933), "It seems to me that psychoanalysis, by inserting the unconscious between what is physical and what was previously called 'psychical,' has paved the way for the assumption of such processes as telepathy."

Or is our search for the mystical another way our brain tries to make sense of the world? Evolutionarily speaking, our survival depended on finding patterns and order in our environment. We naturally look for motifs and meanings to explain the unexplainable; another way of saying this is that we weave together a narrative out of disparate information. In some ways, this is similar to our concept of transference, where we seek to apply what we already know about people and situations, the preordained scripts we all hold, to new situations.

This chapter's vignette may bring into question many of our assumptions about how we come to know something. This story leads us to consider whether there are inexplicable spaces or ways of learning about or accessing another's mind for which we do not have a current explanation. Our author leaves us wondering: How can someone communicate from one mind to another's? Are there close connections that allow for alternative ways of knowing for which science does not account? In "Dreams and Occultism," Freud (1933 [1955]) wrote about these curious occurrences:

> What we call "telepathy" is, as you know, the alleged fact that an event which occurs at a particular time comes at about the same moment to the consciousness of someone distant in space, without the paths of communication that are familiar to us coming into question. It is implicitly presupposed that this event concerns a person in whom the other one (the receiver of the intelligence) has a strong emotional interest. For instance, Person A may be the victim of an accident or may die, and Person B, someone nearly attached to him— his mother or daughter or fiancée—learns the fact at about the same time through a visual or auditory perception.
>
> (36)

Such emotional closeness exists between our author and Kimmy. Despite being years and miles apart, the unbreakable bond remains and reemerges in the dreams.

Similarly, just such an intimate relationship exists between therapist and patient. Indeed, Tiina Allik (2003) notes that the unconscious is always uncanny, framing psychoanalysis as an exploration of the uncanny and the unexpected in life. "Paradoxically, one may need to have a capacity to experience uncanniness in order to discover truly new things about the world" (13). Therapy, similar to any creative endeavor, requires that we remain open to surprise.

In *Who's Behind the Couch?*, Robert Winer and Kerry Malawista ask senior psychoanalysts from around the world if they have ever had an "uncanny experience." All reported some type of unexplainable sense of "knowing." Several spoke of moments in treatment that felt as if they were reading a patient's mind. Jane Kite said,

> I'll never forget this. . . . This was years ago, this was actually before I was in analytic training. I had a young man on the couch, and he was talking away, and I had a note pad, and I found myself drawing a picture which had nothing to do with what he was saying . . . of a haystack in a field, and about three minutes later he started talking about [a haystack]. Is this like telepathy or something?
>
> (Winer and Malawista 2017, 323)

Along the same vein, Nancy McWilliams tells about dreaming in concert with a patient:

> "One night, a Sunday night before [a patient's] Monday session, I dreamed that I was on a canoe trip with her, and I was in the bow and she was in the stern. The canoe looked a little bit like the couch and we're on both ends of it. I'm paddling for all I'm worth, and the canoe is going really, really slowly, and I don't understand this, and I finally turn around and I see her in the back of the canoe. She has shelved her paddle and she's got her arms folded across her chest, and she's just letting me do all the work . . . [When the patient arrived that morning] she lies down on the couch and looks at me and says, 'Over the weekend I went on a canoe trip with my mother.' And then she describes exactly what my dream was. She says, 'I was in the bow, she was in the stern, I'm paddling away for all I'm worth, and the canoe is going really slowly, and I turn around and there she is, sitting

there with her paddle shelved with her arms folded across her chest, and—' And I was disciplined enough not to go, 'You won't believe what I dreamed last night!' She associated for a while, and she said, 'I think maybe it's because I experience you often as like my mother, and in this relationship, I feel like I'm working hard, and you're just sitting there, saying nothing, not pulling your weight.' I thought I was pulling all the weight, I was so interested in this experience of hers, but the paranormal, whatever it was, is too powerful in that instance to ignore. There was some tuned-in-ness." Moments such as these seem eerie, as if the boundaries between us have disappeared, and we are reading the mind of another.

(Winer and Malawista 2017, 197–98)

As therapists, we are listening to our patient's words with both our conscious and unconscious minds. Using our empathic attunement, we may pick up on what a patient is thinking even before he or she says it. Sometimes, that attunement flows in the other direction. A patient might speak about something that we were just pondering, so that we wonder if it is *our* mind that is being read. We readily think of the therapist listening attentively to our patients, but of course, many of our patients have learned early in childhood to anticipate the feeling states of their own parents to predict when an emotional or physical blow might catch them by surprise—a skill they bring with them to therapy, among other places.

In another interview in *Who's Behind the Couch?*, the psychoanalyst Rosemary Balsam tells of a dream she had during her own analysis:

"I had a dream and I was in this little village with cobblestones, and there was something about a clown and then tumbling, and all kinds of things going on at a little fair in the village, and I was describing all the buildings and everything else, and I was kind of merrily going along in this—and [her analyst] said, suddenly out of the blue, 'You *must* know such-and-such a town in Czechoslovakia.' He said it's a town in Czechoslovakia that he once lived in when he was fleeing the Nazis. It was as if I had perfectly described and known this town. But it's one European country I've never been in. It must've been a weird experience for him. I never thought to ask him afterwards."

(Winer and Malawista 2017, 75)

All of these experiences lie in the realm between what is known and unknown, between what is conscious and unconscious. Yet the question lingers for us: how does something transfer unconsciously from the mind of one person to another? How do we know, or think we know, what is in another's mind?

Theoretically we can understand these moments as intuition, exquisite empathy, or transference or, more unconventionally, as telepathy, what Freud called "thought communication" or "thought transference." Christopher Bollas (1987) introduces the idea of "the unthought known," something unconsciously known on a deep, experiential level but inaccessible to *thought* on a conscious level. Like Freud, he sees these moments of understanding as a return to an earlier experience with the maternal figure with whom the "grammar of our being" is laid down, providing the template for self-experiencing with others and with objects. This can evoke a mysterious familiarity or sense of oneness (32). Later, Bollas referred to encounters with "the ghosts of others who have affected [us]" (1992, 59).

In a similar way, Wilfred Bion identifies "beta elements"—psychic experiences that cannot yet be processed by the mind. Thomas Ogden (1994) brings in the idea of the "analytic third," an interpersonal and intrapsychic space co-created by the analyst-patient pair. In the therapeutic space, reverie promotes an intersubjective closeness that can emit an uncanny feeling, a feeling of being strange or alien while simultaneously familiar.

In her book *Extraordinary Knowing*, Elizabeth Mayer (1996a) explores the possibility of the existence of telepathy, an interest that began when her daughter's rare harp was stolen. A friend had suggested she call a dowser—a person that specializes in finding lost objects—to help. As a last-ditch effort, almost as a joke, she called a man in Arkansas, who shockingly identified the exact California street coordinates of where the harp was found. This incident led Mayer to introduce the term "anomalous mental capacities" to describe the unexplainable ways we know things.

> [What] we habitually categorize under rubrics like intuition, empathic attunement, and unconscious communication involve particular cognitive and communicative processes about which our knowledge remains crucially limited. In the effort to expand our understanding of these processes, I will suggest that it may prove useful to look outside our usual database and examine some fascinating if controversial observations gained not in the clinical setting, but in experimental settings.
>
> (Mayer 1996a, 717)

While Mayer admits that we cannot confirm that the paranormal exists, she encourages the reader to remain open minded to its existence.

We need not believe in the paranormal to remain open to what is ineffable, to the mysterious, to the possibilities of unconscious communications that remain without words, that exceed our understanding. Perhaps for our story's narrator, the intense and meaningful friendship was reawakened in the moment of Kimmy's most inconsolable grief. There are inexplicable bonds linking us to those we love. As Hamlet says to his friend: "There are more things in heaven and Earth, Horatio, than are dreamt of in your philosophy."

Indeed, there are bonds that transcend the physical world.

3 ONE PING AT A TIME

My phone pinged, and this text appeared on my screen: "I should be dead! Nobody would even care. You wouldn't care. Don't bother answering me." I sighed, put the phone face down on the table, and considered what to do. This was the fifth such text I had received that day from Nora, after our difficult session the day before. It had been more than a year since Nora's last hospitalization for suicidal ideation, and she had assured me of her safety. So I knew that these messages were designed to get my attention but not to alarm me—I hoped I was right about that.

I'd been working with Nora for over two years, in careful consultation with her psychiatrist. She had had three hospitalizations in short succession. After the third, she had come to my office weeping. "I'm sorry I haven't done any of the things I'm supposed to do. But I'm ready now. Please, I really want your help this time," she had pleaded. "I can't go to the hospital again, I just can't. It's awful there and I'm so ashamed of myself." Glancing up at me, her face wet and streaked with tears, she went on, "When I'm depressed, I think everyone hates me and I don't deserve to live. When I feel better, I know that can't be true. But I can't ever remember that when I'm spiraling."

A recent college graduate, Nora had moved to our city to pursue a master's degree in art and design. She also worked as a hostess in a local restaurant. More often than not, Nora would text me from work, telling me that she was leaving early or skipping work the next day. Schoolwork piled up, as did her incompletes, and she was in danger of being asked to leave her program (and of losing her job). The one thing that seemed to steady her was her passionate interest in photography. Behind the lens, Nora felt free, in control, and exuberant— feelings that were completely new to her. She became caught up in the amateur photography community, using almost every free moment to take pictures or work in the darkroom. When her shoots went well or she succeeded in sticking to her schedule, she felt calm and focused. She sent her photographs to various local competitions, and she was often selected as a finalist. If her plans to work on a new technical skill were derailed, or if a submitted photograph was not selected for a prize, she would spiral into despair, complaining bitterly that she was worthless and deserved to die.

Nora's texts to me came when her self-loathing and sense of worthlessness peaked. In the office together, we talked about what these messages meant to her and to me. What was she hoping I would understand when she texted me like that? What did she think I would do? How might I feel? It surprised her to learn that I felt worried about her, or that I was sorry she'd been having a bad day or a tough photo session. She explained to me that my reactions made no sense to her. "When I feel that way," she told me, "I really don't think you care at all. I can't remember how I feel when I'm here in your office. In my mind, you're mad at me. I can see your face and hear your voice berating me: 'You're nothing! You're no one! Why are you even here? You don't deserve anything good!' But I know that's not how you think at all. I just don't remember that when I'm not here."

One day, Nora's text had a different tone. "Please call me. It's urgent." I called, and when she answered the phone, she was crying, and I could hear the sounds of people talking in hushed tones in the background.

"It's my father," she told me in a shocked tone. "He . . . he had a heart attack in the night. He died. I just can't believe it." She recounted tearfully how the night before the family had been out to dinner together—herself, her two brothers, and her parents. Her father had complained about pain in his abdomen, which he thought was indigestion, so he'd taken some antacid pills and gone to bed as soon as they got home. In the morning, he was dead.

The next several days were a whirlwind for Nora and her family, who were reeling from their father's unexpected death. Nora recounted to me how she and her brothers were planning for the funeral in between managing her father's financial affairs and comforting their grief-stricken mother. "My father was always the one who took care of us," she cried. "Now my mother just sits in her chair. She won't even eat or talk to anyone." In the midst of this turmoil, I began to notice that Nora was functioning very differently. Rather than being paralyzed by grief, she seemed to be the most competent in her family, making the difficult decisions the others could not face, contacting family and friends about the funeral, and arranging many details that escaped the notice of her mother and siblings. In our sessions, she grieved and feared that her father's death was her fault, as though she should have known that his discomfort required medical attention.

Nora asked me to attend the funeral. "I know I'll feel safer if you're there," she said. "I am afraid of giving the eulogy—what if I start to cry? If you're there I'll feel comforted." Another time, she said, "I want you to be there so you'll be able to see all the people I talk about all the time. You'll be able to understand me." I told her that I would attend, recognizing that it was deeply meaningful to her. I encouraged her to imagine what it might be like for me to be with her family— might she feel some discomfort? What were her expectations?

My mind flashed to what she had told me of her early childhood years. Her anxious and preoccupied father had lost his job as an accountant when Nora was four and could not find steady employment until she was in high school; her mother was sad and impassive, perhaps because her own mother had died when Nora was an infant. Her brothers' success at sports and the sciences outshone Nora's artistic endeavors in their mother's eyes. What would it be like for Nora to have me witness the family together, grieving the unexpected loss of her father? Would it impinge on her ability to keep me all to herself, or might she feel embarrassed or ashamed that her therapist was at the service? I reflected privately that showing up at the funeral made me uncomfortable as well, as though leaving my office was like an actor breaking the fourth wall. Was it a necessary action, or would it breach the boundaries of the treatment?

But she was adamant that I attend. Thinking it over together, we recognized that for Nora, my presence at the funeral felt like a necessity, as we had both seen how difficult it was for her to hold me in her mind. Although she was functioning well, I was concerned that the funeral might precipitate another spiraling depression that could land her back in the hospital.

On the day of the funeral, I arrived at the church a few minutes before the service began. When Nora saw me, she ran over to greet me and asked if she could give me a hug. I stood in the back during the service, and, as we had agreed, said a brief goodbye at the end before slipping out quietly. I was struck by Nora's poise and grace as she gave the eulogy, with her brothers flanking her and her mother weeping in the front row.

Over the next several months, there was a distinct shift in Nora's comportment. She spoke about her relationship with her father, a warm and loving parent who had supported her unconditionally even when he did not fully understand the sources of her unhappiness. She was patient with her mother and kind to her brothers. "They just won't talk about it," she told me. "It's like we just can't mention Dad's name. Jeremy will just leave the room, and Jack will usually get mad at somebody or storm away. They just can't talk about their feelings at all."

29

At school, Nora began to complete her assignments and turn in her work. She told me that she now understood what her father had been trying to tell her. "He tried so hard with me," she sobbed. "I wish I could have shown him that I could really apply myself, really do well. I wish he didn't have to die before I could show him that."

Nora continued to submit her work to competitions, but she no longer berated herself when the outcome was not what she had hoped. When she didn't place well in a competition, she expressed disappointment but recognized that she'd have other opportunities.

A few months after her father's death, my phone pinged. I picked it up to see a text from Nora, one that made my heart sink. "I'm nothing!!" it read. "I should just not be here anymore! Nobody cares about me, and you don't either. Don't bother calling me back!" I couldn't believe it. Were we really back there, at the beginning again?

Five minutes later, another ping came. "I am sorry." I lifted my eyebrows. "I didn't mean that. I am upset but I am OK. Can we please talk today?" I breathed a sigh of relief. For the first time, I realized that Nora had been able to keep me in her mind.

I texted back. "Would you be able to talk later this afternoon?"

Analysts Reflect on Mentalization

> There is something at work in my soul, which I do not understand.
> —Mary Shelley, *Frankenstein*

In this chapter's vignette, we meet a therapist disquieted but largely resigned to her patient Nora's distressing text messages, which are *designed to get my attention but not to alarm me*. Nora's therapist has heard Nora's despair before and is keenly aware of the feelings of worthlessness and suicidal thoughts that had previously resulted in hospitalizations.

In a subsequent session, Nora is able to step outside herself and reflect on what she felt when she sent the text. *When I'm depressed,*

I think everyone hates me and I don't deserve to live. When I feel bet-ter, I know that can't be true. But I can't ever remember that when I'm spiraling.

As therapists, we keep our patients in mind, collecting their sto-ries, interactions, and communications, and we draw upon them in our therapeutic exchange. This capacity to hold another in mind is not sufficiently developed in many of our patients. We see this devel-opmental lag when our patients describe their deep-rooted insecurity and instability—not knowing who they are moment to moment.

The concept of mentalization (Fonagy and Target 1998; Wallin 2007) describes this critical transformation we see in Nora. Mentalization—the ability to reflect on our own mind and to under-stand that the other person has a separate mind—emerges gradually in the young child. Developmental psychologists study how children come to understand behavior in terms of mental states, wishes, and intentions in themselves and in others (Stern 1985). Incrementally, a child develops the capacity to see another as having mental function-ing, moving from projecting his own experience onto the other to recognizing—by about age four—that the other might have a differ-ent mental experience (Fonagy 1991).

Let's look more deeply at this important developmental break-through. How *do* we learn to know our own minds? As parents we hold our children in mind from the time they take their first breath. We prepare ourselves for this absorbing parental role before they are born through our fantasies of who our children might become. Indeed, the child's physical and psychological survival depends on this capac-ity to keep the child always in mind.

Children learn to recognize their own mind—to mentalize—through the consistent emotional attunement of their early caregiv-ers, who put into words what the child is thinking and feeling. For instance, a parent, seeing a child pointing to the door, might say, "Oh, I see you want to go outside." This attunement happens over a mul-titude of life experiences as the child gradually comes to know her own feelings and intentions. As Lewis Aron (2000) writes, "I learn to reflect on my mind because another person regards me as having a mind to reflect on, and my discovery of this is a discovery that that person has a mind too, and I only become conscious of myself because someone else takes me to be a self" (675). The infant who looks to the mother to see herself reflected in the mother's eyes begins to integrate this image of herself in the eyes of another (Winnicott 1967).

However, this capacity to hold another in mind is not sufficiently developed in many of our patients. In this chapter's vignette, Nora declares that she is unable to manage her strong emotions or to tame the harsh critical voice inside of her that she attributes to her therapist. Nora's failure to accurately perceive or infer the state of her therapist's mind is tied to her inability to regulate her own affect: *When I feel that way, I really don't think you care at all. I can't remember how I feel when I'm here in your office. In my mind, you're mad at me. I can see your face and hear your voice berating me: "You're nothing! You're no one! Why are you even here? You don't deserve anything good!" But I know that's not how you think at all. I just don't remember that at all when I'm not here.*

Nora holds her therapist in mind only when she is troubled, texting her to report her distress, but is unable to remember an alternative to her painfully dismissive image of her. In our story we observe that Nora's capacity to hold her therapist in mind increases, and she eventually is able to draw upon these internal images for her own self-regulation.

As Sheldon Bach (2001) posits, this essential capacity to hold another in mind is coupled with the capacity to feel that one is remembered by the other. Perhaps Nora's frequent distressed texts represent her dual efforts to place herself firmly in her therapist's mind lest she be forgotten and simultaneously to establish her therapist's presence in her own mind.

Although in the real world, our experience of seeing, hearing, smelling, and touching people guarantees their existence for us, their continued existence when not within the grasp of our senses is guaranteed only by our memory of them. And just as we keep people alive by remembering them, so we sustain feelings of our own aliveness not only through the ongoing awareness of our actual physical beings, but also through feeling that we exist and are remembered in the minds of others.

(Bach 2001, 74)

We learn that Nora is overwhelmed by work and school demands. She is newly excited by photography, but her internal mood is dictated by her successes or frustrations in this sphere. *Behind the lens, Nora felt free, in control, and exuberant—feelings that were completely new to her.* External recognition and success in her art calms her, but when that is absent, it leaves her in an emotional tailspin. *She would spiral into despair, complaining bitterly that she was worthless and deserved to die.* David Wallin (2007) makes sense of this kind of all-encompassing despair: "When embedded in experience, it's as if we *are* the experience as long as the experience lasts" (135). When Nora felt deflated professionally, she became a deflated, worthless person.

Wallin explains, "When we are mentalizing, however, we can ask ourselves just how real or unreal our present sense of our experience actually is" (143). Mentalizing "creates the potential for affective, cognitive, and behavioral flexibility, in large part because it allows us to envision multiple perspectives on any given experience" (136). Without the capacity to mentalize, "unmetabolizable emotions . . . can readily be experienced with traumatic intensity" (Coates 1998, 125).

When Nora's feelings would reach an intense crescendo, she would text her therapist. In a subsequent session, her therapist initiates an exploration of what Nora believes her therapist's reaction might be: *What was she hoping I would understand when she texted me like that? What did she think I would do? How might I feel? It surprised her to learn that I felt worried about her, or that I was sorry she'd been having a bad day or a tough workout. She explained to me that my reactions made no sense to her.*

This therapeutic conversation is significant because it allows Nora to begin to piece together how her therapist's mind works. As with a child who looks to a parent to see herself reflected, that reflection provides room to expand her understanding of her own mind. Sheldon Bach (2001) tells us "understanding how one's mother's or father's mind works is an important task of growing up, and one that has gone awry for many of our patients" (743).

We can assume that Nora suffers from several critical developmental tasks gone awry: her knowledge of her own feelings as dynamic representations in her own mind, her recognition that her therapist might think and feel differently than she expects, her understanding that her own internal experience does not necessarily make it real in the external world, her struggle to know she is carried in her therapist's mind and to hold her therapist with her even when they are not in contact, and her ability to regulate her own emotions.

Susan Coates (1998) deepens our understanding of these interlocking processes. "The child who does not find his or her mind in the mind of the mother is left without an awareness of his or her own mind and without a personalized, authentic, and vitalized sense of self" (124). Like Nora, "A child whose reflective-functioning has remained underdeveloped and compromised by the parents' preoccupations and defenses will be prone . . . to breakdowns in functioning" (123–24).

There are clues here that help us understand the source of Nora's deficits and conflicts. Presumably, her parents, her earliest caretakers, failed to convey that they held her in mind even when she was not present. This disrupted her ability to feel a continuous sense of herself. We know that Nora's mother experienced the loss of her own mother when Nora was an infant and that her father lost his job when Nora was young. It is likely that both parents were overwhelmed with their own losses, distracted by their troubles, and may have been unable to meet the ordinary emotional demands of parenthood.

Bach (2001) explains:

> The child's continuous existence in the mind of the parent . . .
> provides the continuity on which the beads of experiences are strung
> together and become the necklace of a connected life. . . . [T]he most
> difficult therapeutic issues arise in those cases in which the parent
> was emotionally absent or uninvolved, for then the string of conti-
> nuity on which to assemble experience is missing, and the child is
> left clutching a handful of beads or memories that form no discern-
> able pattern.
>
> (748)

It takes steady perseverance and her therapist's compassion to correct the early lapses in attentive parenting that have brought Nora to
this point. Perhaps her father's death allowed Nora to integrate her
father in a new way, by taking on his competence and dedication. As
readers, we may be surprised to read Nora describe her father: *a warm
and loving parent who had supported her unconditionally even when
he did not fully understand the sources of her unhappiness.* And even
more striking, when her father dies, *rather than being paralyzed by
grief, she seemed to be the most competent in her family, making the
difficult decisions the others could not face, contacting family and
friends about the funeral, and arranging the many details that escaped
the notice of her mother and siblings.*

It seems that Nora's sense of the continuity of her own feelings and
experiences and her capacity to know that these experiences can be
and are being held in mind by her therapist contribute to the notable
leaps she makes during this stressful period of her life. Nora is able to
articulate her wish that her therapist attend her father's funeral and
to anticipate how that experience might go. Her sensitive, responsive
therapist goes to the funeral, holding all of what she and Nora know
of each other, thereby supplying a profoundly important necklace of
continuity for Nora.

Central to the curative process, Bach (2001) writes, is that

> the analyst must keep the patient alive in his or her own mind in a
> continuous way, and the patient must believe that the analyst holds
> the patient and keeps him or her alive in memory. Reciprocally, of
> course, the patient must learn to keep the analyst consistently alive,
> and the analyst must feel that he or she remains alive in the mind of
> the patient.
>
> (749)

This is both the developmental aim—and the therapeutic aim—that
is solidified by the time Nora prepares for her father's funeral.

Just months after her father's death, Nora is flooded with affect
and once again texts her therapist. But this time she follows her urgent
text with another: "*I am sorry . . . I didn't mean that. I am upset but
I am OK. Can we please talk today?*" The complex, emotional relationship between Nora and her therapist demonstrates that therapy
can mediate the scars of childhood and bring the patient to health.
"When we help to access, illuminate, and bridge the patient's various
emotions, states of mind, and levels of experience . . . we are strengthening the patient's capacities both for affect regulation and for mentalizing" (Wallin 2007, 148).

For the first time, Nora's therapist tells us, *I realized that Nora had
been able to keep me in her mind.*

4 WHAT ARE YOU THINKING?

"I'm afraid that I will always be alone, that I'll never meet someone to marry. But I have no idea why I feel that way." Those were Rachel's first words when I asked her how I could be of help.

As I sat across from this engaging, attractive, twenty-four-year-old woman, I too wondered why she feared a life alone.

She went on to tell me about a recent breakup with a fellow graduate student she had been dating for two months. He initiated the ending, and she told me that she was not unhappy about losing him: "I was more upset that I had no real feelings for him or any sense of connection." In other words, she was more distressed by the *idea* that she had been rejected and that the rejection had come from an "appropriate, Jewish guy—the type I'm supposed to marry." Rachel added, "For some reason, I have this fear that I won't be loved, which is what I want most in life." She then elaborated a history of short-term relationships with men she found either "appropriate and boring" or "inappropriate and exciting."

The therapy evolved over the next several weeks. It was clear to me that Rachel was not only eager to dive in but that she also had a deep self-reflective capacity. She was open and receptive to thinking about the underlying reasons for her unsatisfying relationships. With this in mind, I recommended that we meet twice weekly.

When describing her parents, Rachel initially focused on her relationship with her father. She described him as her "hero," the "most wonderful man," "a god." She sheepishly added, "I'd like to marry a man just like him." She went on to say, "I always feel loved by my father. I don't know why I think I won't ever be loved." After a long pause and a deep breath, she said, "Maybe he loves me too much."

"Too much?" I asked. She went on, "I was Daddy's little girl," smiling with pleasure as she shared the recollection of her father's adoration and appreciation that she was "pretty *and* smart." She remembered delighting her father by dressing up and performing show tunes. With pride she told me that he hung each of her stellar report cards on his office wall. She tentatively let me know that her father could also be somewhat seductive toward her, and even more hesitantly, she conveyed her own seductiveness with him.

Only in later sessions did Rachel speak of her close relationship with her mother, whom she criticized for being a "submissive housewife." Rachel was disdainful that her mother prepared meals, dressed up for her husband's return home at the end of his workday, and appeared to follow exactly his political and social perspectives. She often fantasized that her father preferred her over her mother, because he doted on her and showed an interest in her ideas. This fantasy left Rachel puzzled, especially when she felt protective of her mother when her parents argued.

When Rachel started therapy, she and her mother were in the habit of talking to each other on the phone every day. During these calls, she'd tell her mother everything she'd been doing, especially intent on giving her all the details of her sexual exploits—late nights in bars and at parties, followed by sex with men she didn't know—edgy encounters that bordered on being dangerous. These conversations always unfolded the same way: Rachel's mother—as one might expect—reacted anxiously to her daughter's uninhibited sex life. "Rachel," her mother would scold, "What are you doing? Are you out of your mind?" In response, Rachel would feel shame and guilt. When these phone calls ended, she'd feel upset and angry. She asked me, "Why does she always have to make me feel so bad about myself?"

Gradually, Rachel began to wonder if there were more complex reasons for these strained phone conversations. Initially she considered whether she was inviting her mother's admonishment for doing things that she too felt uneasy about. Some sessions later, she wondered aloud, "I'm suddenly thinking that maybe I'm hoping to make my mother envious. Maybe that's why I feel so bad all the time, like I've done something terrible, but I just don't know what it is. Maybe I'm really just being mean to her." With surprise, Rachel added that she was often drawn to women she felt competitive with, both at school and socially.

Rachel started to call her mother less often, and she no longer felt compelled to confess her risky behaviors. And without exposing herself to her mother's criticism, she was also feeling less guilty.

During one session, Rachel settled in and remarked, "This week I smoked pot every night. I don't know why; it messes with my school work." Previously she had told me that she sometimes smoked pot to release stress but that she didn't like it and had decided not to smoke it anymore. I wondered aloud why she had started up again now, particularly since she had been pleased that she had stopped. But she seemed to have no interest in exploring it. Instead she went on to tell me of her budding interest in a classmate. Offhandedly she said, "I cut a couple of classes in order to spend time with him."

She continued, "I'm starting to feel like a typical silly girl, only talking about wanting a guy." She knew from her past experience that when she got all "crazy over a guy" she didn't focus on her studies. This, she believed, would render her like her mother, which clashed with how she wanted to see herself. On the one hand, she wanted to be as pretty and feminine as her mother, but on the other, she devalued her mother as a "silly girl" without a career.

Offhandedly, Rachel added, "Oh, yeah, I know I'm changing the subject, but I think I might be pregnant." I thought I glimpsed a bit of a smile as she looked up at me expectantly. Her period was late, and she had not used birth control on multiple occasions when she was with a man she was no longer seeing. "He was such a bad boy! I loved riding on the back of his motorcycle!"

What are you thinking!? were the words that shot through my brain. How could she speak of being pregnant so nonchalantly? I knew she wanted to finish graduate school, and during a previous session, she had talked about how awful a friend's abortion was and that she was in no position to have a child.

I was overcome with uncharacteristic judgment and annoyance at her carelessness. I recognized that these strong feelings were unusual for me in the consulting room. I took a breath, working to keep my bearings. I said, "You look almost pleased, even though you know what a terrible position you'd be putting yourself in." No sooner had the words left my mouth that I felt misgivings. I thought I had contained my reaction, but I hadn't. Rachel lowered her head and picked at her thumbnail. The image of Rachel and her mother talking on the phone popped into my mind. Under the guise of inviting her to explore the denial of her risky behavior, my comment carried disapproval—just as her mother's did.

Regaining my equilibrium, I said, "When you told me you might be pregnant, you felt like you were changing the subject. But right before that, you said that you felt like a silly girl, the way you sometimes see your mother." I paused, gauging her reaction. She was looking at me with interest. I continued, "I'm thinking about what's been happening with us here today. You told me about smoking pot, cutting classes to hang out with a guy, and then the possibility of being pregnant. I started to wonder whether our conversation was beginning to sound like one of the calls you used to have with your mom."

I immediately recognized that my critical feelings had been building, as if I was being filled up with Rachel's previously intolerable shame and guilt. So I posited: "When I said to you that you were putting yourself in a terrible position, it must have felt like I was criticizing you but trying to hide it. I was judging you, just the way your mother does."

"Oh, yeah! You're right!" Rachel exclaimed. "That is so strange. I think a part of me really wants my mother to react badly on the phone, to get her upset, even though I would have said I didn't want that at all. But it also makes me feel terrible. I have been acting out of control. And what if I really am pregnant? That would be awful. I would be a silly girl like my mom. I'd be just like her." She grabbed a tissue, crumpled it in her hand, and said, "Maybe that's my punishment for acting so crazy."

Analysts Reflect on Projective Identification

> It was amazing, when you thought about it, how effortlessly hate slipped into the space reserved for love and vice versa, as if these two things, identical in size and shape, had been made compatible by design.
>
> —Richard Russo, *Bridge of Sighs*

There is a lot that we could unpack in this story. We've decided to focus on the moment when the therapist loses her typical composure, because it offers one way to understand this clinical exchange.

From the very first meeting, Rachel communicated her troubled state of mind and her worry that she *will always be alone, that I'll never meet someone to marry.* She told of being her father's favorite, quickly connecting this to her fear that no partner would ever love her as deeply as he did. *I was always loved by my father. I don't know why I think I won't ever be loved . . . Maybe he loves me too much.*

We learn that Rachel spoke to her mother daily: *She'd tell her mother everything she'd been doing, especially intent on giving her all the details of her sexual exploits . . . edgy encounters that bordered on being dangerous.* Repeatedly she provoked disapproval. When her mother questioned her behavior, *she'd feel upset and angry. She asked me, "Why does she always have to make me feel so bad about myself?"*

In time Rachel no longer felt compelled to tell her mother so many details of her private life. As she no longer felt pulled into such interactions with her mother, the conflict moved into the treatment room. One day Rachel reported: *This week I smoked pot every night*, followed by *I cut a couple of classes in order to spend time with* a new man she was seeing. To each of these revelations, the therapist listened with curiosity, wondering what this meant to Rachel.

A bit later, Rachel nonchalantly said, *Oh, yeah, I know I'm changing the subject, but I think I might be pregnant.* Here the therapist noted a strong internal reaction: *What are you thinking!?* Recognizing this atypical, disapproving response on her part, the therapist offered what she hoped was a neutral interpretation: "*You look almost pleased, even though you know what a terrible position you'd be putting yourself in.*" Yet as soon as those words were uttered, she knew that despite her best effort to hide it, the underlying condemnation had been spoken. Unable to take in and metabolize the experiences that Rachel was sharing, the therapist gave it back to her in what ostensibly appeared to be an interpretation but still contained within it the kernel of criticism she had hoped to filter out. Like the patient's mother, the therapist was feeling what the patient herself could not bear to feel—which is one of the ways we describe the phenomenon of projective identification.

Melanie Klein (1946), who originated the term, described projective identification as an unconscious phantasy in which aspects of the self (an internal object) are split off and attributed to another (an external object).[1] In this case, the projective identification happened when the therapist takes on what Rachel could not bear to recognize in herself.

Breaking the concept down further, projective identification occurs when someone is unable to process some unmanageable affective state or experience and instead places the split-off part into an other, leaving that individual to manage it. The receiver of the unwanted affect takes in the feeling and then feels pressure to act in a way that fits the projection. The person doing the projecting (Rachel) seeks to remain in a close relationship with the other (the therapist). As Sandler (1987) describes it, this relationship gives the individual "the unconscious illusion that one is controlling the unwanted and projected aspect of the self" (40). In this way, projective identification differs from the more straightforward defense of projection, where one parks unwanted parts of the self with another person or group, making them a container for his or her own frightening and unwanted impulses and fantasies. But in projection, instead of staying in relationship with that person/group, the one projecting dissociates from the recipient of the projection. Racism is an example of this type of projection: negative qualities are attributed to a racial category that the projector then wants nothing to do with.

Most theories of projective identification require that the person who takes on the unwanted feelings have some resonance or identification, often called a "hook," with whatever is being projected. Thus projective identification is co-created and arises in an intimate dyadic relationship, such as what happens in the relationship between significant others, between parents and children, between siblings, and between a patient and therapist.

One difficulty with the term "projective identification" is that this ridding oneself of persecutory anxieties is often described as "putting something into an other," which sounds like something out of a science fiction movie, where one invades another's mind and takes control. It is, however, a *metaphoric* transfer of a feeling state into an other. As Edna O'Shaughnessy ([1981] 1988) stressed, this communication occurs unconsciously, in unarticulated phantasy.

Klein (1946) first used the term "projective identification" to describe interactions in the mother-infant dyad as an omnipotent phantasy in the mind of the infant, who at this stage of life and mental development (birth to six months of age) is occupying the early paranoid-schizoid position exclusively. In this early stage, the infant splits the good mother (or "breast") from the bad mother (or "breast"), keeping the source of painful, unmanageable experiences separate from the source of soothing, good ones. Klein refers to this as position as "paranoid" because the anxiety is experienced as malevolent and as coming from the outside. When the infant is able to integrate the good and bad into one mother, a whole object, the infant has attained the depressive position. In the depressive position, the child perceives the risk of losing the loved parent, who is necessary for survival, and begins to grapple with complexity of guilt, mourning, and reparation.

Rachel seemed to straddle both of these positions. She experienced her mother's reactions as angry and revengeful persecutions, which aroused guilt and the fear of losing the bond with her mother. Her phone calls aroused her mother's criticism and concern, even as Rachel unconsciously sought to expel the "bad," or unacceptable, parts of herself and locate them in her mother, in the hope that her mother could more effectively contain and manage those feelings. At the same time, Rachel sought condemnation and punishment from her mother for her actions, which had, in fact, stimulated guilty feelings.

While Klein saw projective identification as a primitive defense, Wilfred Bion framed it as a form of affective communication. In his paper "Attacks on Linking" (1959), he distinguishes between normal and pathological projective identification. Normal projective identification is when a mother/analyst receives the emotional and mental distress of the nonverbal baby/patient, tolerates it or holds it, and responds in a soothing manner, providing relief and containment.

In our story, Rachel's complex affective communication was repeated with her therapist. She projected onto her therapist the internal representation of her mother as a critical, persecutory presence in her inner world. The therapist received the projection and felt similarly pulled to criticize the patient for her risky behavior in the same way her mother had. In essence she was telling Rachel that her feelings were unmanageable, that she could not digest them, give them back to her in a new form, or take in the deeper meaning of the communication.

Only after the therapist recognized what was happening in the room was she able to contain the feelings and offer them to the patient in a form she could understand and work with:

> "When you told me you might be pregnant, you felt like you were changing the subject. But right before that, you said that you felt like a silly girl, the way you sometimes see your mother." I paused, gauging her reaction. She was looking at me with interest. I continued, "I'm thinking about what's been happening with us here today. You told me about smoking pot, cutting classes to hang out with a guy, and then the possibility of being pregnant. I started to wonder whether our conversation was beginning to sound like one of the calls you used to have with your mom."

The therapist needed first to notice her internal reaction and then, as Bion (1963) described, take in the projection, contain the feelings, and instead of responding punitively, put the interaction into words, allowing both patient and therapist to begin to understand and explore the exchange's meaning. The therapist was able to pivot from the position the mother had been locked into, thereby opening up more space for the patient to access the full range of her internal experiences.

It is this containing role on the therapist's part—to reflect, rather than withdraw or retaliate in the face of the patient's destructive feelings—that both allows for and promotes the patient's ability to think—to move from feelings that are in the body to thoughts that are in the mind.

Bion gives the example of a hungry infant crying for the breast. Crying is a way for the baby to be understood, to communicate to the mother, nonverbally, the raw emotion (what Bion calls "beta elements"), with the hope that the mother understands the unspoken in the same way. When the infant is faced with overwhelming, confusing, and unmanageable anxiety and lacks other means of coping, the mother can organize the baby's experience. She transforms the experience, metabolizing and digesting the beta elements into something manageable for the baby (alpha elements), and then communicates to the infant that she understands his needs and will attend to them. It is the mother's capacity for containment and reverie, like the therapist's, that enables the infant to recognize his needs and begin to think about them.

The therapist in this story needed to be receptive to Rachel's projections and to respond in a way that interpreted to Rachel what was happening in the room, without giving back the unmetabolized reaction—the therapist's initial response. Bion recognizes that no mother will be a perfect match for an infant, just as no therapist is a perfect match for a patient. In good-enough mother/child and therapist/patient relationships, there is the opportunity to revisit and repair moments of rupture and use them productively.

There are other ways to look at this interaction between Rachel and her therapist. For instance, we might view it through the transference lens, in which a patient repeats with the therapist, or "transfers" onto her, whatever wishes, desires, and fears she has experienced in earlier relationships. One could say that Rachel transferred onto her therapist the disapproving mother, which served as a way for her to ameliorate her guilt, and, at a deeper level, hide her competitive urges and wishes to make the mother envious.

Likewise, the therapist's response could be understood as a countertransference one. Freud understood countertransference as the analyst's unresolved transference (conflict) with the patient. This creates a blind spot in the analyst, something necessary to overcome for the analysis to proceed. Using Racker's (1957) early description of countertransference as either "concordant" or "complementary," we could say that this was a complementary countertransference response, that is, one in which the therapist identified with the patient's internal objects (the mother), as opposed to concordant countertransference, in which the therapist identifies with the patient.

Different versions of these interactions repeated over the course of the treatment. The therapist's deepening self-awareness kept her from being swept up by the patient's projections. With consistent empathic interpretation, Rachel took ownership of her distressing feelings. She was able to recognize and own the pleasure she felt in letting her mother know she was attractive to men, with the hope of arousing her envy. In time, her risky behaviors diminished and she allowed herself to enter into a loving and enduring relationship.

5 THREE MORE DAYS

"Give me that," Nellie snarled. "You can't play with it."

Startled, I paused my lunch preparations to listen more closely to the exchange between my five-year-old daughter, Nellie, and Marisa, her best friend since age two, in the next room playing. Marisa practically lived at our house. The two girls were typically sweet natured and kind to each other.

"Get your own Pretty Pony," Nellie said.

For the third time this morning, Nellie sounded like a tyrant. What was going on with her? Did I need to intervene? Again? I peeked into the playroom. In a warning voice, I said, "*Nellie.*" Usually hearing me say her name in that tone was enough to set things right again. Marisa stood before me, her eyes wide, looking as shocked as I felt.

For the past few days, I had been baffled by Nellie's cruel treatment of Marisa. She was saying things I had never heard from her before. Nellie was always one to share, offering the bigger half of a candy bar to her friend.

It was Sasha, Nellie's older sister, who was the bossy one. Yet no matter how bossy or territorial Sasha was being, Nellie adored her.

She accepted all of Sasha's rules—dominance was a small price to pay to be near her. Now that Sasha was at a one-week sleepaway camp, I had imagined I would get a break from the demands and taunts I often heard when my daughters played together.

When Nellie's aggressiveness first started, Marisa came to me in tears, telling me that Nellie was being mean to her. I pulled Nellie aside and reminded her that Marisa was her friend and guest and that she needed to treat her kindly. Yet the next day, Nellie was even more unrelenting in her teasing and bullying. I was stunned, wondering what could make Nellie turn so fiercely on her beloved friend. Now it had been consecutive days with no relief for Marisa, and she asked me if she could go home. Marisa never wanted to go home early.

Hoping my stern look and saying her name would snap Nellie back, I returned to the kitchen to pour two glasses of milk. I was about to call them to the table when I heard Nellie say, "You're not doing it right. I said, *don't* touch it." Then I heard Marisa start to cry. Nellie's voice turned mean, "You are such a *cry baby*. Whaa, whaa, whaa." Suddenly, I recognized that voice. It wasn't Nellie's voice; it was Sasha's: Sasha's Bossy Big Sister voice.

It occurred to me that Nellie had barely mentioned Sasha since she left for camp. How had I not noticed that Nellie wasn't begging for Sasha to come home? There had been so many evenings during the school year when Sasha would go to a friend's house to work on a school project, and young Nellie would spend the hour or two she was gone repeatedly crying, "Where's Sasha?" Her father and I would distract her for brief periods, usually by him playing his guitar. It worked for a minute or two, but pretty soon Nellie was back to asking, "Where's Sasha? I want Sasha," finally settling down when Sasha walked in the door. It hit me then: rather than missing Sasha, Nellie was *being* Sasha.

I called Nellie into the kitchen. This time, instead of talking to her about the way she was behaving, all I said was, "Nellie, do you miss Sasha?"

Nellie's eyes widened like she suddenly remembered something, and after a brief pause, her face crumpled, and she began to weep. Weep and weep. I hugged her tight and said, "I know you must miss Sasha so much."

Nellie shook her head yes, and through her tears she said, "I want Sasha to come home. I want Sasha."

"I know how much you love her," I said (and thought, but didn't say, and how much you love Marisa). Pointing to the calendar, I showed her which day Sasha would return. "How many days is that?" I asked.

Nellie climbed up on my lap and together we counted, "One, two, three," our voices rose with the final number: "Three!" Nellie smiled up at me.

"See, just three more days," I reassured her.

Grabbing a crayon, Nellie drew a big pink star on the calendar square, marking the date when Sasha would return. Satisfied, she climbed down from my lap and returned to Marisa. "Here," she said, handing Marisa the Pretty Pony. "You can play with it."

Analysts Reflect on Identification

Henry Jekyll stood at times aghast at the acts of Edward Hyde.
—Robert Louis Stevenson, *Dr. Jekyll and Mr. Hyde*

In this chapter's vignette, we consider the role of identification in maintaining a relational tie, the power of a meaningful intervention, and the impact of siblings on friendship. In our story we observe a young child's effort to work through her feelings of missing her older sister. Nellie's mother, initially perplexed by her daughter's unusual behavior, soon recognizes that Nellie is outwardly treating her friend in much the same way her big sister Sasha treats her. In other words, with Sasha being away, Nellie is behaving *like* Sasha in order to hold her close and soften her feelings of loss.

We all imitate or incorporate aspects of those we admire—like a respected parent or teacher or colleague. It is perplexing when we take on an unadmired characteristic of another. In our story, without being conscious of it, Nellie models the harsh behavior associated with her sister's treatment of her. Why would Nellie treat her friend Marisa in the same cruel manner in which she herself had been treated? As we attempt to make sense of Nellie's taunting, the psychoanalytic concept of identification is useful. Freud ([1922] 1955) writes, "Identification is known to psychoanalysis as the earliest expression of an emotional tie with another person" (105)—an unconscious mechanism that links two people together. When Nellie behaves like Sasha, she is linked to her, keeping the relationship alive, even when Sasha is away.

Identifying with another not only secures a bond; it also allows for the mastery of external circumstances that are troubling (A. Balint 1943). When Nellie takes on a characteristic of her sister, whom she misses, it allows her to feel some control over her strong but unconscious emotion, and with that control, she can console herself. Alice Balint offers another example of consoling identification when she describes a young boy who is angry about having to leave his beloved dog. The boy switches from playing happily with the dog to yelling at it, saying, "Horrid dog! I don't love you!" Balint explains, "Here we can see plainly that the child was angry with the bad dog that was the cause of his sorrow at parting" (99). Just as we see with Nellie, this boy transforms the painful, distressing experience of leaving his dog and makes it more tolerable through his anger and rejection. Interestingly, Balint observes that this type of identification can result in the repetition of an interaction in "a more merciless fashion than the child himself actually experienced [originally]" (105). This speaks to Nellie's behavior toward her friend, which exceeded the cruelty that she had received earlier from her sister.

Nevertheless, it is perplexing that Nellie treats Marisa so mercilessly. To understand Nellie's aggressive behavior, we turn to Anna Freud's (1937) original ideas about "identification with the aggressor."

She posits that children attempt to master the discomfort or anxiety they feel at the hands of an aggressor by behaving in play much like that aggressor, thereby transforming distress into a feeling of security and control. As many parents can attest, the line between an older sibling's bossiness and bullying can be murky, and a child's reenactment of that aspect of the sibling relationship can shine a light on it. Nellie converts her sorrow at missing her big sister into the fierce teasing of her sister-substitute Marisa. *"Give me that,"* Nellie snarled. *"You can't play with it."* Here we see that Nellie identifies with Sasha's cruelty toward her, channeling her internally while missing her in the external world. Nellie's identification with Sasha mitigates the pain of her absence.

In psychoanalytic literature, the term "identification" (Koff 1961; Foreman 2018) is obfuscated by overlapping and contradictory explanations of its mechanisms and effects. However, there is wide acceptance that identification is important for maintaining a relational bond and for managing the uncomfortable feelings engendered by a more powerful and threatening person. Identification with an aggressor is common, and it plays out in many relationships in which we might accommodate another more powerful person at our own expense (Frankel 2002). We see this aspect of identification in Nellie through her mother's report that *no matter how bossy or territorial Sasha was being, Nellie adored her.* Accepting all her rules and *dominance was a small price to pay to be near her.*

There is a personal cost to this identification with an aggressor: it requires that we subordinate our feelings (Ferenczi 1933; Frankel 2002). By pushing away our own feelings, we can instead focus on what we imagine the other—the aggressor—might be thinking and feeling. That way we can anticipate an attack and behave compliantly to ward off additional aggression. For Nellie, by identifying with her sister and thereby preserving their bond, she unwittingly risked her friendship with Marisa.

While some theorists (A. Freud [1933] 1966) refer to identification, others use the term "introjection" (Ferenzci 1909; Frankel 2002) when describing the dynamic of taking the aggressor into one's own mind and behaving toward others as that aggressor has. "Introjection is certainly involved when a child takes on an attacker's badness, because such a child internalizes and rearranges the actual abusive events in her mind to make herself the cause of her own abuse. This grandiose sense of control is preferable to facing the reality that she is a helpless victim" (Frankel 2002, 108). In other words, it was unconsciously preferable for Nellie to copy Sasha's mean behavior than to miss her (and Sasha's mean behavior) and feel helpless for doing so, or to be angry with her for that mean behavior, at the risk of reprisal, thereby jeopardizing Nellie's important bond with her older sister.

A nuanced analysis of "pathological identification" suggests that identification is a way to avoid consciously remembering hurtful or neglectful behavior by another, preserving the parent—or big sister, in this case—as good, "internalizing or identifying with them" (Foreman 2018, 20), and protecting the perpetrator from anger. In our story, we see that Nellie is not conscious of behaving like her big sister; nor does she feel any anger toward her. Her underlying feelings center around missing her. *Nellie's eyes widened like she suddenly remembered something, and after a brief pause, her face crumpled, and she began to weep. Weep and weep. I hugged her tight and said, "I know you must miss Sasha so much."*

The process of identification is linked to the contemporary relational position that we all have a multiplicity of self-states (Mitchell 2000). We assimilate aspects of others, and these characteristics contribute to the myriad states of mind in our different relationships and in our personal character and ideals. While Nellie's identification with Sasha likely does not represent her ideal self, it does reflect a quality of her personality—an example of one of her many self-states. When Nellie torments Marisa, both her friend and her mother are taken aback. This particular state of mind in Nellie is unfamiliar to them, yet it clearly corresponds to something internal in her: *She was saying things I had never heard from her before. Nellie was always one to share, offering the bigger half of a candy bar to her friend.*

The mother's awareness of her daughters' sibling dynamics allowed her to understand that Nellie, missing her sister but unable to access those feelings or put them into words, had identified with her sister, effectively *becoming* Sasha. Indeed, this is what Freud (1921) posits: in order to retain a tie to another person internally, we "become" that person, leaving them intact externally. Nellie's mother does not jump in prematurely to punish Nellie or to separate her from her friend. Although she *was stunned, wondering what could make Nellie turn so fiercely on her beloved friend*, she intuitively understood that there was something important being expressed by Nellie's atypical behavior. By musing about the dynamic of adoration and bossiness that characterized the relationship between her two daughters, she realized that Nellie hadn't been talking about her absent sister the way she normally would. Instead, Nellie's mother approaches her daughter tenderly. *This time, instead of talking to her about the way she was behaving, all I said was, "Nellie, do you miss Sasha?"* Nellie's strong reaction confirmed what she suspected: *her face crumpled, and she began to weep. Weep and weep.*

What was it that made this mother's comment have such a remarkable impact? Her words worked like a magic salve, linking her daughter's unspoken feelings about her sister to her aggressive behavior toward her friend. And with this linkage, the pressure released, and Nellie began to cry. As analysts, we know to pay attention to our internal musings when treating our patients. We are curious about something our patients say or do, we mull it over in our minds, it comes together in an idea, and we pose it to our patients. Then we await our patient's response, which may or may not validate our interpretation.

If our interpretation is correct, we see "an increase in the patient's insight or emotional introspection, the emergence of new associative material leading into deeper layers of the patient's mind, and changes in the patient's symptoms and behavior" (Kernberg 1994, 1193). Therapists do not simply attend to the patient's words and respond to them; they also attend to the patient's response to their interventions, "tracking the interpretative sequence" (Lichtenberg 1992, 272) to determine whether expanded awareness follows the therapist's comment. In this chapter's vignette, the link that the mother draws between Nellie's hurtful behavior toward Marisa and Nellie's sadness in missing her big sister is validated by Nellie's response to her interpretation. *Nellie shook her head yes, and through tears said, "I want Sasha to come home. I want Sasha."* After they together mark the calendar to see when Sasha will return home, Nellie *climbed down from my lap and returned to Marisa. "Here," she said, handing Marisa the Pretty Pony. "You can play with it."*

The taunting ceases, and as if by magic, Nellie's sweet temperament returns.

By the time we get to the resolution in this story, we have watched Nellie's mother proceed from confusion to clarity about Nellie's bullying behavior. In listening to our patients, we rely on our sensitivity, or, as Patrick Casement (2006) describes it, our "clinical antennae." He writes: "I have tried to develop a similar sensitivity, trying to listen to my own 'footsteps' in a session, listening to how a patient was responding to my own input from moment to moment" (161).

Like an attuned therapist, Nellie's mother pays attention to her daughter's words, discerned the communication her words belied, and listened for Nellie's reaction to her interpretation. Nellie doesn't know why she is mean to her friend. Her mother gradually recognizes that Nellie's behavior is her way of communicating her sad feelings about her sister's absence. *Suddenly, I recognized that voice. It wasn't Nellie's voice; it was Sasha's: Sasha's Bossy Big Sister voice. It occurred to me that Nellie had barely mentioned Sasha since she had left for camp. How hadn't I been surprised by this lack of attention to Sasha's absence?* Putting Nellie's sadness into words allowed her anger to subside.

In this story, and with the insight provided by Nellie's mother, we see how identification plays out specifically in a sibling relationship. While psychoanalytic theory has generally overlooked sibling relationships in favor of examining parent-child relationships, we know

55

from clinical experience that siblings can play an enormous role in our patients' lives, yielding both "nourishing and pathogenic potential" (Agger 1988, 5) for development.

Sibling relationships are affected by birth order, gender, rivalry, loss, concern, aggression, identification, and the ways that a parent views a particular child—something most of us understand from personal experience or clinical anecdote. Older siblings have an impact on the tensions around separation and individuation in younger siblings (Leichtman 1985), which influences identity formation. Both positive and negative feelings form the foundation of sibling relationships throughout childhood and, indeed, throughout one's life. Sometimes, we choose friendships that echo the pattern of our sibling dynamics (Agger 1988). In therapy, discussing sibling dynamics can surface material in the patient that was previously unconscious.

The relationships between Sasha and Nellie and between Nellie and her friend Marisa highlight these ideas. Nellie's mother observes her *sweet-natured and kind* daughter become *unrelenting in her teasing and bullying* of her best friend. Frustrated that she would not have the hoped-for *break from the demands and taunts* while Sasha was away for a week, Nellie's mother recognizes that Nellie sounds just like her big sister. Nellie patterns her taunts of Marisa after Sasha's taunts of her, repurposing the dynamic between sisters to the relationship between friends.

As analysts, and as parents, we understand that behavior—even disruptive behavior—is a form of communication.

PART TWO
Development

6 WHAT LURKS UNDER THE BED

"Oh, thank you so much for calling me back so quickly; Kate and I are exhausted," Julie told me over the phone. "Max, our three-and-a-half-year-old, is all of a sudden not sleeping, even though he has always been a good sleeper. I don't know what the matter is. He seems terrified. We are at our wits' end. Can you see Max?" I could hear both warmth and distress emanating as we talked.

I suggested that she and her wife schedule a time for us to meet together, to talk further about Max and his worries. "Without Max?" she inquired with surprise.

I explained that in situations involving a young child, I prefer to meet with the parents first. I want to learn everything I can about the child and to get context and history. I couldn't yet know what the treatment would look like, but I knew the place to start was with the parents. "I know quite a bit about what young children might worry about, but you both are the experts on Max," I explained to her.

I arranged to meet with Julie and Kate the following week while Max was in morning preschool. Sounding calmer, Julie thanked me as we hung up the phone.

The young couple, huddled together on my couch, smiled nervously. From the dark circles under Julie's eyes I could tell that Max's sleep issues hadn't changed much since our phone conversation.

"Hi, I'm Kate—Max's other mom." After a pause, she added somewhat apologetically, "We've never talked to a therapist about Max before. Where should we start?"

"At the beginning!" I said. I wanted to hear everything about Max.

Julie pulled out her phone, proudly showing me a recent picture of a cute, curly-haired little boy with bright blue eyes and a mischievous grin.

"What a great smile!" I said.

I could tell at once that Julie and Kate had spent a great deal of time preparing for our meeting. They spoke easily about Max and about their relationship, Max's conception story, and his early developmental milestones. I wanted to hear about when the sleep troubles first began. Had there been recent changes at home, I wondered? Were there other signs of stress?

Bit by bit, a story began to emerge. Julie (whom Max called Mima) worked part-time from home and provided most of the during-the-day care of Max, and Kate (whom Max called Mom) was a lawyer who had her own practice (outside of the home). They had never worried about Max before, as he had always seemed to thrive. He made friends easily with boys and girls, some from the preschool he attended three mornings a week and others from the neighborhood. Kate proudly reported that all of his teachers spoke of how bright Max was and that he was especially good at building things out of blocks.

From everything they told me, Max was a healthy, well-developed three-and-a-half-year-old boy with two parents who clearly adored him.

I invited his parents to tell me more about Max's "sleep troubles." They relayed that he was scared of both the dark and of monsters. Tearfully, each night, he implored Julie (Mima) to sit on the edge of his bed until he fell asleep, clutching her hand. If Kate (Mom) offered to give Julie a break, Max pushed her away and insisted that only Mima would do.

Recently, whenever he woke up in the middle of the night, he would scream in terror and beg his parents to let him sleep in their room—which they sometimes allowed, so that they could get some rest. They had no idea why Max's fears had erupted. He had always been a child who fell asleep on his own with relative ease. His bedtime rituals of reading stories and the comfort of his "blanky" had been all Max needed to drift off to sleep.

I asked them to tell me how he liked to play and what he liked to play with. They said that lately he was obsessed with a game of shooting Mom, pretending to kill her with a water gun. Kate laughed, describing the elaborate drama of falling to the floor amid her son's gleeful giggles. She added, "It's a game he could play all day long!"

After the first information session with Julie and Kate, I suspected that Max's sleep problems were a normal developmental bump in the road. I decided I could best help these exhausted yet thoughtful and motivated parents by providing an overview of Max's developmental challenges. With support, reassurance, and guidance, the three of us could help Max manage his fears.

I suggested that Julie and Kate ask Max whether there was something in his room that made him feel afraid. They were surprised to realize that they had been so focused on getting him to sleep each night that they had never asked Max this important yet basic question. They agreed to explore this during the following week.

At our next meeting, Kate and Julie said that Max had declared that he was afraid of the big green monster living under the bed. Knowing this would certainly not completely resolve the problem, I offered a simple yet often-successful remedy for a pesky under-the-bed monster: a spray bottle filled with water and labeled "Monster Spray." I suggested they invite Max to join them in vigorously spraying underneath his bed.

The following week, Julie and Kate let me know that the "Monster Spray" had worked wonders and that Max enjoyed the power of vanquishing the monster beneath his bed. With the enthusiasm of budding detectives, they reported that Max had offered some valuable clues: that he was terrified of his toy tyrannosaurus rex, with its sharp claws and teeth, and also of his towering NASA missile. Although these toys had been in his bedroom since he was a baby, Max now saw them as dangerous.

Together we imagined the many ways that Max might be transforming these playthings into scary objects. I suggested Kate and Julie encourage Max to make up stories about his toys that would allow us to better understand what they represented to him. From there we could try to help him resolve those fears through play.

A clear picture of Max's worries gradually unfolded, and he now had a new use for his water gun: he would shoot Kate with it and then become the doctor who would heroically save her. This expressive play offered a window into Max's internal world. I explained to them that a child Max's age has many reasons to feel angry toward one or both parents, because they set limits or curb his autonomy. In Max's case, he had a particularly strong bond with Mima and was very possessive of her. Once his parents better understood Max's developmental stage and his fears, they became less worried. Settling down for bedtime—for all three family members—was no longer fraught with distress.

Soon Max initiated a new nightly ritual. In his pajamas, teeth brushed, he'd carry the dinosaur and rocket down the hall to the guest bedroom, set them on the dresser, and shut the door. Returning to his room, he'd spritz under his bed with "Monster Spray" and hop into bed. With that routine established, he was able sleep without Mima sitting right next to him. Every morning, Max would march back down the hall and retrieve the dinosaur and the rocket. In the light of day, he no longer feared those sharp teeth and that powerful missile—but he still locked them securely in the guest bedroom at night.

Analysts Reflect on Childhood Fears
and Separation Anxiety

> There's a monster under my bed. I can hear him breathing. Listen.
> I told you. There's a monster under my bed. . . . What if my foot
> slips over the edge while I'm asleep? He'll bite it off, that's what.
>
> —James Howe

Most parents are familiar with a young child's fears of monsters, ghosts, and threats lurking under the bed. Fear is an inborn biological response and an evolutionarily constructive one. While these fears can seem irrational and at times crazy-making for parents, they are a healthy and adaptive way for a child to make sense of their world. Can you imagine the dangers for a developing child if they completely lacked fear?

When the therapist suggested that Julie and her wife meet together with her, the surprised mother asked: *Without Max?* Our clinician believes that parents know their child best and that meeting with them alone would offer enough support and information to dispel some of the tension in the family and enable the parents to engage with the problem in a new and creative way. With insight into Max's struggle, they could provide the ongoing support he needed without him entering into therapy.

In the first parent session, the therapist learned about the monster living under Max's bed and offered *a simple yet often-successful remedy for a pesky under-the-bed monster: a spray bottle filled with water and labeled "Monster Spray."* Why did she offer a spray when she knew perfectly well that the only monster was in Max's imagination? The answer lies in her understanding of child development and how children think. "Monster Spray" works for the same reason that Max was afraid of monsters to begin with. Children of Max's age see the world through a lens of their wishes and fears. It is a time of wonder, imagination, and creativity, when thoughts and fantasies seem magically real. In this world of "magical omnipotence," Max believes there *are* terrifying monsters under his bed, and he is convinced that the magical spray *is* powerful enough to vanquish them.

The author writes: *I suspected that Max's sleep problems were a normal developmental bump in the road. I decided I could best help these exhausted yet thoughtful and motivated parents by providing an overview of Max's developmental challenges. With support, reassurance, and guidance, the three of us could help Max manage his fears.*

In order to assist Max's parents in providing him with the protection and abstract thinking that he was not yet capable of, the therapist encouraged them to enter Max's world of make-believe to help him conquer the monsters from within and progress on his developmental journey.

In the second session, Julie and Kate reported, with the *enthusiasm of budding detectives*, that Max was *especially afraid of his toy tyrannosaurus rex, with its sharp claws and teeth, and his towering NASA missile. Although these toys had been in his bedroom since he was a baby, Max now saw them as dangerous.*

Max's diffuse fears at bedtime, previously allayed by a transitional object (his blanky), had now become located in his dinosaur and NASA missile. The therapist understood that bedtime was also a significant moment of separation for Max, one in which he clung tightly to Mima for comfort. Such moments of separation are particularly frightening for a child—after all, in a world where magical thinking prevails, anything can happen.

Max's new fear of his familiar toys falls along a developmental continuum that includes the use of a transitional object—in Max's case, his blanky—which *had been all Max needed to drift off to sleep.* The transitional object preserves the soothing function of the mother while apart from her. At the same time, it effectively produces a sense of security for the child, who can now feel he has control over an external object even though he has no control over his parents, who can come and go. As the child develops past the stage of the transitional object, he or she becomes aware of complicated ambivalent feelings toward important people.

Without the maturity or psychological resources to anticipate danger and self-soothe in an anxiety-provoking situation, an infant or young toddler might rely on a transitional object to magically bridge the space between the need for internal soothing and the demands of the external world.

We can view Max's recent fears as another means of coping with separation. But at Max's stage of development, the wish to preserve the needed relationship is accompanied by the recognition that he could lose his parents or their love. The three- or four-year-old child has more complicated, and sometimes conflicting, feelings than the younger toddler, including intense love, rivalry, and anger at feeling his independence thwarted by limits setting. By diverting his ambivalent and angry feelings away from his parents and onto his toys, Max maintains a loving and seemingly conflict-free connection to his parents. No longer diffuse and overwhelming, the frightening feelings he imagines present in toys can be controlled and removed from his room.

While we can never be certain of the source of Max's anxiety, his parents noted that it coincided with the expression of strong feelings of attachment to Mima at bedtime and intense rivalry with Kate seen in the onset of his imaginative play: *shooting Mom, pretending to kill her with a water gun.* This upsurge of aggression toward Kate, in concert with his deep love for her, could have produced enough anxiety to result in his recent separation fears.

In the same way that a transitional object is a replacement for the soothing function of a parent when apart, Max's bedtime fear of his toys was an attempt to preserve the relationship to his parents by positioning his anger and anxiety outside himself and divert his destructive feelings away from Mom. Both transitional objects and childhood fears protect the infant and child and enable them to titrate anxiety and avoid panic.

The use of transitional objects and the development of childhood fears reflect a child's natural, healthy growth. They are universal attempts at mastery, which contribute to the development of psychological defenses and secure protection from separation anxiety. These processes provide the child with an external way to provide mental structure and regulation before the cognitive and emotional advances that arise internally as they age. "Winnicott described a healthy developmental progression that runs from babies' devotion to their transitional objects to their emergent ability to play (1953) to their development of the capacity to be alone ([1958] 1965) and to their possession of the ability to participate fully in the life of their culture (1967)" (Malawista et al. 2011, 59).

Once Max's parents understood that their son's worries were fundamentally healthy, they became less worried themselves. Max located his fears in objects he could understand, control, and literally see—successfully circumscribing his fears and keeping them from overtaking his life. Simultaneously, his fears successfully kept his parents close to him at a developmentally vulnerable moment, which reassured him that he wouldn't lose them, while concurrently protecting them from his aggressive impulses.

7 BUTTERFLY BANDAGE

It was a warm day, and my friend Tracy and I were in my backyard on our Whirly-Bird—a self-propelled, horizontal merry-go-round, acting like little kids again. We sat across from each other, pumping our arms and legs as hard as we could, spinning, spinning, until everything blurred.

Rusty, my dog, was having fun chasing me, nipping at my shoelaces. Then the Whirly-Bird lurched and stopped. The center pole had snapped, and the jagged end of it flew through the air to where my hand was pumping, slicing off the tip of my index finger. Tracy's eyes expanded, and her mouth opened in a wail, registering the cut before I did. Bright drops of red blood dripped down my finger and landed on the white cement, spreading slowly outward.

My head was already spinning, but now I was lightheaded and felt like I might faint. I jumped off the Whirly-Bird and started to run up the stairs, until I was hit by the sudden and shocking realization that my mother was not inside waiting for me. No mom who would know what to do. No mom to take care of my cut. My mom had died. Just months earlier, smashed in a car, my little brother, terrified and hurt, wailing in the backseat.

My mind was a jumble. What do I do now? Where do I go?

"I don't know what to do," I said out loud. Then I remembered hearing that a week earlier, a family had moved in across the street, and the mother was a nurse.

I took my chances and headed across the street. I rang the doorbell. A woman with dark hair, big twinkly blue eyes, creamy skin, and—like my mother—a few extra pounds promptly opened the door. "Hello," she said.

I held my finger up for her to see. "Oh, my!" she said. "What happened to you?" Her voice was warm and welcoming. She smelled like babies—a mix of Johnson & Johnson baby powder and Desitin. There was a juice stain on her white nurse's uniform, which I was happy to see—the uniform, not the stain.

My finger throbbed with each beat of my heart.

She asked me my name, and when I said "Jody," she told me that I could call her Juliette. I liked her already (grownups almost never said I could call them by their first name). I followed her into the kitchen.

Juliette introduced me to her kids. Ben was coloring at the kitchen table. One-year-old Sebastian was sitting in a high chair eating Cheerios. It was like walking into my house, months earlier.

But it was their mom, not mine, who held up my hand to stop the bleeding.

"Let me have a peek at that finger," Juliette said. She grabbed a couple of napkins and gently put pressure on the cut. There was something about her command and comfort that brought tears to my eyes.

"Well," she said, as she wrapped my hand in a kitchen towel, "let's get that fixed up for you." The phone rang, and Juliette answered it. I stared, transfixed, watching her finger twirling the cord as she spoke, that same way my mom had. They both had the same shape of face, the same blue eyes. She told whoever was on the other end of the line that she had to get off. "I have a child to take care of."

"Wait here, I'm going to get my supplies," she said, as she walked down the hall. When she returned, she wrapped her arm around my waist and ushered me over to the sink. "I'm going to clean it," she said as she opened the bottle of peroxide. "Sorry, it might sting a bit."

"I don't mind," I said.

After she looked carefully at my finger, she fixed me with her lightly etched eyes and said, "You know, we should get you to the hospital for a few stitches."

"Hospital!" All I could picture was my brother's three-year-old body near death, tubes sprouting out of his arms and chest, and hearing his cries down that long hall. I pleaded with her not to make me go there.

"Well, maybe a butterfly bandage will hold it together," she said. Did she know what had happened to my mom? I let out my breath—I hadn't realized I was holding it. As she pulled the bandage out of the box, I could see that it really did look like a butterfly: thin in the center, spread wide on both ends. The center part stretched over the cut, and the outside wings pulled tight, so that the cut stayed together.

When she finished dressing my finger, we sat talking at the kitchen table. I imagined we were two moms getting together for an afternoon chat, just like my mom used to do with her neighbor friends. Juliette asked, "How old are you, anyway?" When I told her almost twelve, she said she would have guessed at least thirteen. "You're pretty smart for your age." I felt as if I were standing under a piñata, with candy raining down around me.

I turned up on Juliette's doorstep the next day and most days after that. Juliette always answered the door with a big smile, looking like I was just the person she was waiting to see.

Analysts Reflect on Mourning in Children

> The loss of the daughter to the mother, the mother to the daughter, is the essential female tragedy.
>
> —Adrienne Rich, *Of Woman Born*

In this story we see a moment when the reality of Jody's mother's death comes crashing through her twelve-year-old defenses. Not surprisingly, it occurs at a moment of injury, a time when a child ordinarily turns to her mother for comfort and aid. *I was hit by the sudden and shocking realization that my mother was not inside waiting for me.*

After losing a parent, a child naturally wonders how she will survive. Here Jody collected herself and sought comfort and connection with someone like her mother. We can see her quick thinking as a way to protect herself from the acute awareness that her mother was truly gone: an attempt to avoid the reality and magnitude of her loss. Rather than missing what she couldn't have, Jody quickly found an alternate mother to tend to her.

Child theorists explore, and often debate, the developmental thresholds children need to cross to be able to truly mourn, and some maintain that mourning isn't possible until late adolescence. Adding to the debate is how mourning differs from grief. Our current understanding of the distinction between mourning and grief is based on inferences drawn from infant observation. John Bowlby (1960), a pioneer in the field of infant attachment and loss, writes that when children even as young as six months of age lose their primary attachment figure, they show signs of anger, sadness, anxiety, or trouble with sleeping or eating. In many ways, these are the same initial reactions that we see in adults. Yet what Bowlby is describing may not actually be mourning—the ongoing process set in motion after a loss—but the early expressions of grief. Grief is seen in all humans, and in all mammals, when they experience a significant loss. Such grief reactions may even precede the developmental capacity to recognize that a person still exists even though they are out of sight, what we refer to as object constancy. It is likely that with recent developments in neuroscience, we may be able to gain an understanding of how grief manifests itself at an even earlier developmental stage.

Freud ([1917] 1955) describes *adult* mourning as the bit-by-bit, painful, and slow struggle to accept a death or loss, which includes a gradual withdrawal from the other and a willingness to find comfort and relationship elsewhere. If we think of mourning as this "bit-by-bit" withdrawal of the attachment and the acceptance of the reality of the loss, then mourning is not possible for a child. How could a child, like Jody, de-attach from someone who is basically an extension of herself and integral to helping her negotiate every aspect of her daily life? If a parent dies, the world is irrevocably changed in the most fundamental and devastating of ways. As Rita Frankiel (1994) writes, the child's "need for nourishing interaction and care . . . is so central to the survival of young children that the withdrawal necessary for adult mourning is simply not possible" (328).

Altschul (1988) describes the work done at the Barr-Harris Children's Grief Center, which confirms that a child's mourning does not form a straight line; the process shifts and changes based on the development of emotional and cognitive growth. From the perspective of research on adult attachment, we understand that "the processing of these early experiences [of childhood trauma] is an essential factor in integrating the loss, in gaining new meaning, and subsequently creating new relational bonds" (Ringel 2019).

Mourning, then, is a more complicated ongoing process than grief, requiring a higher level of cognition and abstract thinking. To mourn, one must first be able to truly comprehend death and loss. The question then arises: at what age does a child have the cognitive ability for such abstractions and an understanding of the finality of life lost? The age many researchers pinpoint ranges from six to nine years old (Smilansky 1987). Even though Jody at age eleven can accurately recount the details of what happened to her mother and verbalize her distress, she could not completely accept and integrate the full meaning of the loss.

Children cannot tolerate or sustain inconsolable pain, which may threaten to overwhelm them. The ability to bear such a devastating loss emerges over the course of maturation as they begin to make sense of the world and their own experience in it. For this reason, it is not surprising to see children, right after learning of a significant death, simply return to their play. They may not even cry. Most children are eager to resume their regular activities, at school and with friends, seeking a quick return to "normal" life. In reality, nothing will feel quite "normal" to them for a very long time, try as they might to hold on to life-as-they-knew-it. This may explain why many therapists and writers attribute this lack of affect to children's inability to mourn. "Lack of affect in a grief reaction should not be conflated with the emotional resilience required for mourning" (Ringel 2019). As Robert Furman ([1968] 1994) notes, when adults are exposed to the poignancy and pain of a child's mourning, "they prefer for their own sake to deny its existence" and instead see the child as not in mourning (374).

Another common reaction after the untimely death of a parent is silence, which may also reflect a more general denial. Francine Cournos (2001), both an analyst and memoir writer, describes her family's desire to protect one another from pain after the death of her father. She writes, "Throughout this entire series of events, my mother and I maintained a pact of silence. As a child, I believed this protected us, and that we would simply fall apart and stop functioning if we discussed our experiences with illness and death, however obvious their impact on our lives" (137). Older children and adolescents may also be praised for being "strong" and "keeping it together," relieving other family members from having to worry about how they are faring.

As therapists, we often treat adults who come to us with some difficulty, seemingly unrelated to the fact that they lost a parent in childhood. The patient may have no difficulty articulating the narrative and details surrounding a parent's death. Yet as the work deepens, we often hear about the unconscious fantasy that the parent left them, often because they were "bad." In this fantasy, the parent is still living in some faraway place and will one day return to them. With further exploration, we can see the many ways that this unconscious fantasy has influenced the patient's life and may actually be connected to their current difficulties. So while it may appear that an adult has acknowledged and mourned the absent parent, he or she may not have truly accepted or integrated the loss.

The form grief takes will depend on where the child is developmentally. Jody at eleven has the capacity to understand that her mother is dead and will never return. Yet she maintains the fantasy that her mother may still be alive when she runs into the house seeking her help. Like adults, children often anticipate they will "fall to pieces" and be unable to regain a sense of control. Jody experiences this sense of overwhelming panic: *My mind was a jumble. What do I do now? Where do I go?*

An older adolescent, capable of higher abstract reasoning, will show more adult-like grief and mourning, particular to their stage of development. For example, an adolescent girl, starting to grapple with issues around female identity, would feel lost without a mother to show her what it means to become a woman. Adolescence is a time of separating from one's parents—rejecting their values, refusing their support, acting out, or other forms of rebellion—in order to establish one's separate identity. If a parent dies during this period, mourning and grief are even more complicated: any friction or conflict in the relationship can no longer be repaired, and the teen will have to resolve guilty and angry feelings.

As children mature, their memories and knowledge of and relationship to the deceased parent often remain sealed off at the age they were when the death occurred—there are no new memories or experiences to update the relationship. In many cases, this can lead to an idealization of the parent rather than a full picture of who he or she actually was, adding to the difficulty in mourning. When someone dies prematurely and is idealized, they remain frozen in time, forever the all-loving parent of early childhood.

For a child to thrive after a significant death, he or she must have the support and care of a reliable surviving parent or relative and the chance to mourn and express their sadness in their own way over time. The surviving caretaker must be able to tolerate the child's sad and painful feelings, letting them know it is okay to be angry or sad. Children need permission from the grownups around them to mourn.

Children often have the ongoing wish to refind the lost parent in fantasy. For example, a child may seek a surrogate parent to provide needed nurturing. This stable, loving figure allows the child to begin to feel that it is safe to love again, without the fear of loss. Jody delights in being cared for by her neighbor, particularly because she reminds her of her mother.

Erna Furman (1981) has written:

> When an adult is ready to reinvest his love, he can actively seek a new person. The child cannot do that, particularly when he wants a new parent. . . . A parent who is well known and loved will forever be missed to some extent with each new developmental step. . . . A parent who is hardly known accompanies the child throughout life differently, but remains as meaningful.
>
> (172)

When Jody sits chatting with Juliette, she is identifying with her mother, and in that way both holding on to her and mitigating the loss of missing her. *I imagined we were two moms getting together for an afternoon chat, just like my mom used to do with her neighbor friends.* Another way the child may attempt to control their over-whelming feelings is by taking on some of the tasks and roles of the deceased parent. Freud ([1922] 1955) wrote, "Identification is known to psycho-analysis as the earliest expression of an emotional tie with another person" (105). After a loss, the expression of this tie becomes even more compelling and necessary. In that moment, the child need not miss the dead parent—she *becomes* the parent.

Juliette provides some of the direct comfort Jody hungers for. We appreciate that Jody could use this positive relationship with Juliette as a way to help ease the pain and loss of her mother. *I turned up the next day, and most days after that. Juliette always answered the door with a big smile, looking like I was just the person she was waiting to see.*

Grief and mourning can last a lifetime. Like Jody in this chapter's vignette, children who encounter such a crushing loss will reexperience this loss over and over (Garber 2008). Jody will feel it throughout the arc of her development—when seeing a warm exchange between a mother and daughter, when she herself reaches certain milestones and accomplishments, such as graduation, marriage, or having a child.

A grief relived, again and again.

8 SAVING SWIFTY

Tommy was an inquisitive and energetic third grader who came for therapy twice a week. He filled our play therapy sessions with tales of robbers, explosions, and car crashes. In all of these tales, he was the hero who rescued the trapped, defenseless girl from death.

After a while, the stories shifted from a hero saving a girl to an older brother rescuing a younger sister. In this version, Tommy offered the sister a perilous situation to navigate, and each time the older, stronger brother would arrive to save her. One of his favorite scenarios was when his house catches fire and he jumps on the fire truck, climbs the ladder, and pulls the terrified little sister to safety.

Tommy had been referred to me for therapy because of difficulties at home and at school. His parents described him as loving and bright, but he had a quick temper that got him into trouble. His parents pointed out that despite "being a handful," Tommy was always kind to his five-year-old sister, Bess. His mother liked to imagine Tommy and Bess being close friends in adulthood—in stark contrast to her own relationship with her older brother. She mentioned how awful it would be if Tommy grew up to be like him.

Four months into treatment, Tommy changed the setup for our play. Upon entering the consulting room, he retrieved the game of checkers from the toy shelf and invited me to join him. At the beginning, Tommy played by the rules, but soon he was jumping my pieces in "illegal" and random ways and making more and more wanton moves. Eventually, he was jumping my pieces every which way.

"Wow, your pieces sure are beating mine," I exclaimed.

"Your guys are just not that lucky, I guess," he responded with feigned innocence.

"Geez," I replied. "My pieces don't stand a chance."

After one particularly complicated move—his checker jumped across the entire board *and* back again several times—he laughed with maniacal pleasure.

"It's so exciting to be able to make up the rules," I said. "You can go anywhere you want in this game and always win!"

Tommy replied, "It's great. I'm sick of rules! Everywhere I go, I'm told what to do and what I can't do." Then he deepened his voice, scrunched up his face, and said, "'You can't do that! Don't touch that!'" I remarked that he sounded like an angry grownup.

"Yeah!" His voice rose in anger as he busily captured all of my pieces till not one remained on the board. "The grown-ups say when I have to go to bed. When I can watch TV. When I can hold the chinchilla."

"You get really mad when you're told what you can and can't do," I said.

"I get *really* mad."

Once he calmed down, he said, "You know when my uncle comes to visit, he always wants his way. We have to eat what he wants for dinner and watch the movie he wants to watch. He's always like that. He is hard to be around. My mom gets really mad at him. She loves her brother, but he makes her furious."

"How can you tell?" I asked.

"You can see it in her face. He drives her crazy! She tries not to show it, but you can see her getting really mad. She could *kill* him she looks so mad." He went on to list some of his uncle's troubling attributes and then repeated, "But he knows she still loves him."

"I guess he's glad to know she still loves him, because he could really worry when she looks so mad, like she could kill him. He might worry that she didn't love him."

"Yeah, he might think that, but he knows she does. He's her brother. You *always* have to love your brother. You have to! But I think after he's at our house awhile she wants him to leave. To get out."

"Wow, she gets so mad she'd like him to get out."

"Yeah, cause he always wants his way. He can be such a pain." Tommy imitated his mother's annoyed voice. " 'He's driving me crazy,' and 'How long is he going to stay this time?' " Then, tentatively, Tommy said, "My sister drives me crazy too. I could kill Bess. I'd like to kick her in the butt."

This was the first time I had heard Tommy openly express anger at his sister. Cautiously, he scanned my face to make sure that I wasn't disapproving or angry. Then he listed all the things Bess did to make him mad, especially that she wouldn't let him touch her chinchilla, Swifty. I raised my eyebrows, knowing that Tommy had his own chinchilla, Oscar.

"But I know how to get back at her. I tell her I am going to sit on Swifty or strangle him, because she makes me so mad. I say those things because it really upsets her. I say 'I'll kill Swifty.' " Once again, he guardedly looked up at me.

I said, "Then you can feel like you're the powerful one, getting her upset, rather than her upsetting you."

"Yeah." He grabbed hold of a stuffed dog. Shaking it by the neck, he said, "I hold Swifty up and I say, 'I won't give him to you.' I can torment her back since she torments me. I hold the chinchilla up by his neck, like this. Bess is so annoying. I can't stand her."

While a part of me wondered whether this was an opportunity to explore what his sister might be feeling, I held back, wanting to give him the space to tell me about his anger. "When you get so mad and frustrated you want to find a way to be strong."

"Yeah, I sure do." Tommy stood up and went to the toy shelf and retrieved the fire truck, the focus of his rescue fantasies. "Where do you get these?" he asked. "I've never seen them anywhere. These really are great trucks." As he raised the ladders, he said, "Wait, you know what? I think I saw one of these when I was three." He drove the fire truck across the couch. "Yeah! You know, I think this is the *exact* same one." His voice softened. "I think Bess gave me one of these trucks when she was born. They are really cool. It had real lug nuts. And look here, you can open the hood and see the engine."

"You sure remember a lot about that truck."

"The truck was from Bess," he repeated. "Well, I guess my Mom actually bought it," he smiled at me and rolled his eyes. "But it was supposed to be from Bess when she was born. I think they also gave me the toy Busy Town." A scowl crossed his face.

"They bought you something because Bess was born."

"Yeah, what a dirty trick! I wanted to bite her I was so mad. Before her I got all the attention. I got whatever I wanted. I got way more as an only child. Now everything has to be *fair*. Fair, fair, fair. I hate fair! I don't want her here. I don't want it fair. I *hate* having a sister."

"Things sure were spoiled for you when Bess came."

"Yeah, and they don't even take away her allowance when she does something wrong! I hate her. I really hate her. I hate having a sister. They kept saying it's so *nice* to have a little sister. How *lucky* I am." He gave a little sarcastic laugh and went on. "Lucky, huh! I didn't want her. I didn't ask for her. It is *not* nice. I'm *not* lucky. I always wanted a brother though. A brother my exact age, always someone to play with. I'd never be lonely if my friends weren't over. We would like to do all the same things. I'd like that. Or an older brother, who could help me, teach me things. Even a younger brother would be better than a *sister*. I could teach him things. But instead I got a sister. Instead I got her . . . Satan's daughter." He laughed. "I got that line from a movie." Putting the fire truck aside, he returned to the toy shelf.

"Oh, yeah, I got my violin today. I'm going to be in an orchestra at school." Tommy spoke of his friends also in the orchestra and the instruments they were going to play. I noticed that Tommy was taking a breather from his intense anger at Bess. After a pause, Tommy crossed the room and picked up the Hess space shuttle from the toy shelf, making it spin straight up into the air. "Did you know the space shuttle goes around like this? It has black tiles all along the bottom so that when it comes back down into the atmosphere it won't burn up. If it didn't have the tiles, the spaceship and crew would burn up."

I was amazed at all the safety details he knew. "It's good to know the engineers do so many things to keep the crew safe," I said.

"And they always replace all 3,047,000 tiles after each trip."

"So no matter how many tiles burn up, they can always get it right again," I said.

"Yeah. My dad and I are going to Florida for a space launch. We're going in May cause that's when the launch happens. I hope we can see the control room."

"Nice to be just the boys together," I said.

"Yeah, not my mom. And *definitely* not Bess."

Analysts Reflect on Sibling Rivalry

> We can count on so few people to go that hard way with us.
>
> —Adrienne Rich

One of the most powerful stories in the Bible is of Cain killing his younger brother, Abel, the perceived favorite of his father, Adam. It is the story of the rivalry, envy, and savagery that can exist between siblings.

Most parents are uncomfortable imagining their child feeling such animosity and rage toward another of their offspring. So when a child says that he "hates" his younger sister or "wishes she was dead," many parents instinctively correct him, saying something like, "You don't hate your little sister! You love her."

At the start of treatment, Tommy's parents denied that there were any issues between their two children. They claimed that they were extremely close and hoped they would become lifelong friends. Tommy echoed this view of the relationship in his early play, where he repeatedly *offered the sister a perilous situation to navigate, and each time the older, stronger brother would arrive to save her.*

There is little in the psychoanalytic literature on the sibling relationship; the primary theoretical focus has been on the parent-child relationship—in particular, early attachment theory and the oedipal forces. Yet siblings can have as much influence on a child's development and identity as a parent. Historically, the "sibling's lateral relations were seen more or less as a displacement of these vertical arrangements" (Balsam 2013, 36). Sabine Trenk-Hinterberger (2014) highlights the many ways that the "horizontal relationship" to a sibling is "often as powerful a psychological force in one's life as a mother or father" (184).

Since her birth, Bess has played an essential role in Tommy's development. Equally important are the three years Tommy had before she was born. Susan Sherwin-White (2014) claims that any new addition to a family results in a shift in each family member's role, evoking complex feelings on both a conscious and unconscious level. When Bess was born, Tommy became aware that he was not his parents' exclusive love. The loss of his parents' time, attention, and adoration generated complicated feelings of rivalry and anger: *They kept saying it's so nice to have a little sister. How lucky I am . . . Lucky, huh! I didn't want her. I didn't ask for her. It is not nice. I'm not lucky.*

Fearful of losing his parents' love, Tommy initially pushed away his shameful, angry feelings and used the therapy to play out rescue fantasies. This allowed him to feel like the hero in his mother's eyes, the good son, and at the same time express some of his aggression by placing the girl (his sister) in increasing danger.

It was only later, when Tommy felt safe with his therapist, that he began to express his wish to be dominant and to display his hostility and aggression, evidenced in his jumping the therapist's pieces in "illegal" and random ways. There was omnipotent delight as he triumphed and captured all of the therapist's checkers. He reveled in the power he felt at not having to follow the rules set down by adults. He may also have wanted to turn the tables, to have his therapist feel what he felt, to experience firsthand the pain of being the *unlucky* one, the one on the losing side.

Tommy openly complained about the many restrictions placed on him by his parents: *The grownups say when I have to go to bed. When I can watch TV. When I can hold the chinchilla.* His therapist responded: *You get really mad when you're told what you can and can't do.* When Tommy confirmed his rivalrous feelings—*I get really mad*—he was immediately reminded of his mother's conflicted relationship with her brother. Tommy knew on some level that his mother was afraid he would turn out just like him.

Tommy might have heard this comparison explicitly stated over the years, because he was well aware of the negative association. Children are often assigned roles in a family based on characteristics, both positive and negative, that are identified with a particular relative. The unconscious messaging can heighten the pressure on a child to behave like that individual. Similarly, children can be encouraged or limited by labels—such as "sporty," "musical," "smart," "moody," or "difficult"—all of which can heighten rivalry between siblings and restrict the potential of the child who is not assigned that particular positive trait.

When asked how he knew his mother felt conflicted about her brother, Tommy said: *You can see it in her face. He drives her crazy! She tries not to show it, but you can see how mad she is getting.* Tommy reassured himself that despite his mother's anger, she still loved her brother: *My mom gets really mad at him, she loves her brother but he makes her furious. But he knows she still loves him. It's her brother. You always have to love your brother. You have to!*

Unable to find a comfortable place to land in the space between love and hate, Tommy feared that his expressed animosity for his sister would lead his mother to want to be rid of him just as she wished to be rid of her brother: *But I think after he's at our house awhile she wants him to leave. To get out. She could kill him she looks so mad.* We could imagine that a frustrated mother may have given Tommy that same look and reinforced Tommy's worry that his bad behavior would lead to his mother preferring his "good" little sister over him.

Tommy unleashed more of his anger: *My sister drives me crazy too. I could kill Bess. I'd like to kick her in the butt.* He then revealed the sadistic pleasure he derived from torturing Bess's chinchilla so that he could feel in control and torment her. This may also have been a way to keep his sister safe from his rage by redirecting it toward the chinchilla. Tommy experienced powerful rivalrous feelings, yet he sensed his mother's equally powerful prohibition. His therapist told him: *Then you can feel like the powerful one, getting her upset, rather than her upsetting you.*

Melanie Klein (1940) addresses the wish to be all-powerful. She writes:

> Omnipotence, however, is so closely bound up in the unconscious with the sadistic impulses with which it was first associated that the child feels again and again that his attempts at reparation have not succeeded, or will not succeed. His sadistic impulses, he feels, may easily get the better of him. The young child, who cannot sufficiently trust his reparative and constructive feelings, as we have seen, resorts to manic omnipotence.
>
> (132)

In Tommy's early play, he repeatedly attempted reparation by saving the sister whom he had put in danger.

It was not surprising that after Tommy expressed his raw, angry feelings and his wish to kill Bess and her chinchilla, he returned to the fire truck to undo the fantasied damage. Seeing that his therapist understood his angry feelings and didn't judge him, he was able to link the fire truck to the birth of his sister. He recalled his delight that she had given him such a wonderful gift, yet now he recognized that his parents were pulling a fast one, hoping to circumvent his jealousy and rivalry.

Rivalry and jealousy exist in triangular relationships when there is competition between two for the desired one. Differentiating envy and rivalry, Rosemary Davies (2018) explains that envy seeks to destroy, whereas "in rivalry, there is a need to keep the object alive, despite the ambivalent tie to the object" (265). Healthy rivalry between siblings can lead to a competitive bond and foster growth. Siblings need to know that it is safe to compete, and to fight with each other, without a parent stepping in to referee and stop the conflict.

Tommy needed to voice his pent-up rage toward his sister so that he could shift to a healthier rivalry. When consulting with parents who are puzzled by their child's jealousy of a younger sibling, we try to help them see it from the child's point of view. For example, how would they feel if their spouse decided to bring home another partner—someone who will share their clothes, belongings, even their bedroom, reassuring them that "you will love them" or, since "I love you so much, I'm getting another one just like you." Most will laugh in recognition at how horrifying a prospect that would be. Bruno Bettelheim (1976) offers another medium— fairy tales—to help children and parents understand the hidden jealousies and rivalries between siblings, and he advocates that children should have the opportunity to voice their conflicted feelings.

While brothers and sisters are rivals for their parents' love and attention, we recognize that love and generosity can coexist with rivalry. In this story, we heard the hate and envy Tommy felt for his sister, but we also saw his urge to protect her. Juliet Mitchell (2003) describes the "duality of adoration and murder" between siblings. Freud ([1900] 1953) too recognizes these competing feelings when writing about his sibling-like relationship with John, his one-year-older nephew:

All my friends have in a certain sense been re-incarnations of this first figure. . . . My emotional life has always insisted that I should have an intimate friend and a hated enemy. I have always been able to provide myself afresh with both, and it has not infrequently happened that the ideal situation of childhood has been so completely reproduced that friend and enemy have come together in a single individual—though not, of course, both at once or with constant oscillations—as may have been the case in my early childhood.

(483)

Freud's tendency always to have an "intimate friend and hated enemy" continued into his professional life with colleagues like Carl Jung and Wilhelm Fliess.

With adult patients, even when a sibling is not overtly the focus of the treatment, we hear traces of these relationships when they speak about the other patients we treat or the ones with whom they cross paths in the waiting room. Some may speak of them as rivals or of their wish to be viewed as the "better," more loved patient; others may develop an affectionate, protective attitude when they see a patient leaving the office crying.

Therapy gave Tommy the opportunity to express what he had lost with the arrival of his sister and his feelings of jealousy and hate, all without the fear of retribution or punishment. As Melanie Klein (1940) writes: "If . . . the mourner is able to surrender fully to his feelings, and to cry out his sorrow about the actual loss there is a relaxing of the manic control over [his] internal world . . . and goodness and love [are] increasingly experienced within" (142).

Tommy's session with the space shuttle and all of its magnificent safety features reassured him that he had not caused irreparable damage, which allowed for ambivalent feelings to coexist within him. It is only when feelings of love and hate can be borne simultaneously that an enduring bond can be formed, opening the door for a healthy rivalry, one that promotes growth and achievement that can be carried into adulthood.

9 BETRAYAL

"Why did you do it?" Leslie sobs, burying her face in her father's chest. "Why did you leave me? I always tried to make you happy, but I know I wasn't good enough."

"Shh, shh, Leslie, that's not true," her father whispered softly. "That's not it at all. Remember what I told you—it's between your mother and me, it's not you. I never want you to think this is your fault or that I'm leaving you. I'm never leaving you, Leslie."

Watching the pair, I was surprised at Leslie's father's gentle tone and solid presence. Rather than deny his actions or shy away from her accusations, he leaned in closer, patting her back softly and soothing her with his calm words. This was not the man I'd expected to meet.

Three weeks earlier, thirteen-year-old Leslie had discovered her father's infidelity when he left his e-mail open on his computer, where she did her homework. Confused and overwhelmed, she showed the e-mails to her mother. Her mother, enraged, enlisted her daughter's help to hunt down more "evidence" against her father. It was the discovery of the e-mails and the chaos that followed that brought Leslie to therapy. This was our fourth session.

"When my mother told my father that she knew all about what he'd done," Leslie confided in our first session, "she went totally batshit on him. They thought I couldn't hear them, cause I was upstairs in my room, but I heard every word. My father didn't even answer any of her questions. He just kept saying, 'Frannie, you need to calm down, so we can talk things over.' 'Talk things over?! Not happening, dude!'" Leslie paused, remembering how her mother snapped at her father scornfully. "He moved out that same night. When were they supposed to talk?" Then her eyes had filled with tears. "But I don't understand it," she said, looking bewildered. "Why is he leaving me? Why wasn't I good enough for him?"

After her father moved out, Leslie began to feel anxious and nauseated, torn between her alliance with her mother against her father and her fear that she was betraying the father she once adored. Until this session with her father, she had refused to see him and wouldn't answer his calls. Although both parents had joined together to reassure Leslie, their only child, that her father still loved her, she persisted in feeling that she was the jilted one.

I could see that she felt powerless. But withholding her love from him hurt her also. For weeks, she remained stuck in this embattled place, neither giving in to his pleadings nor turning away entirely. Eventually, she demanded to know all of the details of the affair but then became enraged at him when he answered her questions. She threw herself headlong into her social life, pretending nonchalantly to her friends that her father was away on an extended trip.

Watching Leslie's struggle to make sense of the ruins of her previously intact family, I, too, tried to make sense of the story. I sought a coherent narrative, but the pieces kept shifting. I wanted an annotated cast of characters: Who is the Good Guy here? Who is the Bad Guy? My mind wished for order, for reason, for clear demarcations, even as my clinical ear was attuned to the subtle nuances of Leslie's gradually unfolding grief.

At first, listening to Leslie rage against her father, I saw him through her eyes—he was the Bad Guy. He was the one who had left a long and committed marriage and child, he was the one who had cheated, and he was the one who had moved out rather than trying to work things out. Not only had Leslie overheard her mother's pleas for couples' therapy; she also had played the role of confidante to her mother, who turned to her young daughter for comfort. It seemed that for her mother, Leslie's discovery of the e-mails made them co-conspirators. Her mother would cry and rage to Leslie, pouring out the details of all that her marriage lacked. In turn, Leslie added her own complaints about her father—she couldn't talk to him, he didn't understand how depressed she really was, he only tried to put a bright face on things. He wouldn't acknowledge the damage this separation had wrought. When I met with Leslie's mother at the initial consultation, I found her sympathetic and empathic to her daughter's pain.

I had listened carefully to Leslie's distress during our first sessions together. But during the third session, she confided that she had long known her parents didn't belong together. "Here's how I know," she said quietly. "Once, when my class had an all-family ice-skating party, I saw my best friend's parents glide along the ice together, holding hands and laughing." She looked up at me sadly, then went on. "When I saw that," she told me, "it dawned on me that I had never seen my own parents do anything like that. They don't even touch each other really—just a peck on the cheek for special occasions."

"I wonder what you think about that?" I asked her.

"Well, my mom is—sometimes she's just in a really bad mood, and if he tries to touch her she yanks her hand away as if she thought he was—I don't know, like gross or something! I always wondered why she was so mad at him all the time. I figured he must have done something to really piss her off."

As I listened, I found my own thoughts shifting, wondering if it was Leslie's mother who was the Bad Guy. I noticed my heart start to harden a bit toward the mother—perhaps it was she who couldn't be patient, flexible, or loving toward her husband, who was a caring father. Perhaps she was the one who had let the marriage deteriorate?

As I noticed my perspective waver and grew more aware of my desire to identify who was Good and who was Bad, I recognized that I was experiencing firsthand Leslie's painful dilemma. Like Leslie, I felt as though forging an alliance with one meant loosening my grip on the other. Yet Leslie required the attention of both of her parents. As a young girl facing a family that was collapsing around her, she needed her parents to put her first, to protect her from their turmoil, and reestablish clear boundaries between them and her.

When Leslie asked if she could invite her father into a session with her, I agreed, but I braced myself, fearing the worst. As I watched them sit on the couch together, Leslie suddenly seemed much younger to me, more like a child seeking reassurance from a difficult-to-please parent. I could see how much she wanted and needed her father.

"Can't you just tell me about what happened?" she pleaded. "Are you in love with that lady you were e-mailing? Don't you love Mommy anymore?"

"Leslie, of course I do," he replied at once. "I will also always love Mommy, because she's part of you."

"But what about your girlfriend? I saw everything in your e-mail!" she said sharply, her voice rising. "I saw your phone too! Those texts and those stupid photos. I can't pretend like I didn't see it! How am I ever supposed to trust you?"

I watched him pause. While he gazed at his daughter, his own eyes filled with tears. "Leslie," he finally said to her, in a low, steady voice. "I am not going to tell you all about the things that happened. It wouldn't be fair, and more importantly, it wouldn't help you or change anything about what happened. What I did was wrong; there is nothing I can say that will ever make it right. I understand that you can't trust me right now, but I hope that you'll trust me again one day, over time. I want to sort this out with you and figure it all out."

"Figure what out? Do you mean you might get back together with Mom?" The words tumbled out in a rush, and I could feel the tension in Leslie's body—was it possible?

Leslie's father glanced up at me, and I took in his pained expression, his shame, and his silent question to me: *Should I tell her the truth?* he seemed to be asking me. I nodded my head slightly: *yes.*

"Leslie," he said, "I do love you very much, and I want you to feel like you can trust me. I don't want to pretend that things will be the same as they were before. I don't think Mommy and I will get back together—not now and not later either."

Leslie slumped back against the couch and let her hair fall over her face. Together they were silent for a very long time, their hands locked together but their gazes averted.

Analysts Reflect on Adolescent Derailment

> In this way, in increments both measurable and not, our childhood is stolen from us—not always in one momentous event but often in a series of small robberies, which add up to the same loss.
>
> —John Irving, *Until I Find You*

In this chapter's vignette, we are ushered into a dysfunctional family drama that eclipses a girl's stable world. Leslie is sobbing in her father's arms as they sit together in her therapist's office. Weeks earlier she had stumbled upon her father's adulterous e-mails, told her mother, was commandeered into finding more incriminating information, overheard her parents' tense arguments, and ultimately lost trust in her father, who soon moved out.

A girl's adolescence is an emotionally turbulent "kaleidoscopic period" (Ritvo 1971, 241), as the hormonal balance shifts and the body changes. As a thirteen-year-old, Leslie was likely just starting to explore her own feelings about love, sexuality, and intimacy and attempting to become her own person, one more separate from her family than ever before. Although a younger child might not consciously register disturbing events taking place in the family that they could not comprehend, Leslie has already begun to traverse the territory between childhood and adulthood, which includes her burgeoning sexuality. The intrusion of her father's affair and his betrayal of his wife and marriage confuses Leslie on both conscious and unconscious levels and threatens to derail her developmental path.

When our story opens, Leslie appeals to her father in stage-characteristic, unfiltered agitation: *Why did you do it?* she wails. *Why did you leave me? I always tried to make you happy, but I know I wasn't good enough.* We appreciate that Leslie's questions swirl with her confusion and that they reveal to her father that she feels betrayed yet responsible for his emotional well-being. Her self-esteem takes a hit.

In her novel *Disobedience*, published more than twenty years ago, Jane Hamilton (2001) writes of a teenager discovering his mother's infidelity when reading her e-mail on the computer he has set up for her. Like Leslie, he must find a way to integrate his punctured image of his straying parent.

> To picture my mother a lover, I had at first to break her in my mind's eye, hold her over my knee, like a stick, bust her in two. When that was done, when I had changed her like that, I could see her in a different way. I could put her through the motions like a jointed puppet, all dancy in the limbs, loose, nothing to hold her up but me.
>
> (39)

As therapists, we often see the damage of technology and social media on the lives of our patients. These platforms can generate envy, breach privacy, and reveal secrets not meant to be exposed. They also provide the opportunity to know more about others' lives than is healthy. In Leslie's story, we see that technology makes deceit harder to conceal.

Leslie's father attends her therapy session at her request, hoping to reestablish their healthy relationship and to comfort her with his presence and with the truth. *Remember what I tried to tell you before—it's between your mother and me, it's not you. I never want you to think this is your fault, or that I'm leaving you. I'm never leaving you,*

Leslie. While we understand the intention behind her father's words, Leslie's father does actually leave her—he has moved out.

Jane Hamilton's teenage character expresses how ineffective parental efforts are to reassure.

> When well-mannered, liberally educated parents get divorced, they are usually quick to assure their children that the split had nothing to do with them, that Mom and Dad had insurmountable problems with one another, et cetera. Any child worth his salt knows this is a matter of horseshit. Parents get divorced because they cannot stand to have one more family dinner together.
>
> (2001, 32–33)

Leslie feels that her father has left *her.* She feels so much shame and confusion about her father's departure and his deceit that she, too, conceals the truth, *pretending nonchalantly to her friends that her father was away on an extended trip.*

Kerry and Jack Novick (2013) describe in their model of working concurrently with parents of adolescent patients that treatment contains "the dual goals of restoration to the path of progressive development and restoration of the parent-child relationship" (103). With those goals in mind, Leslie's therapist works with Leslie and her father to help them contain the emotional upheaval of their relationship. *Can't you just tell me about what happened? Are you in love with that lady you were texting? Don't you love Mommy anymore?. . . How am I ever supposed to trust you?*

At first, Leslie's father seems to forget that she is still a child. Leslie has already suffered from having too much power in the family by discovering her father's secret. Plead though she may, she still reacts angrily when her father answers her questions with more detail than is appropriate, recognizing—albeit unconsciously—that she is not yet at an age when she can comprehend the complexity of her parents' marriage. But Leslie's father regains his equilibrium and reestablishes himself as the father of a thirteen-year-old, treating her as the already-overloaded young teenager she is.

The therapist in this story is surprised by Leslie's father's understanding and kindness. *Rather than deny his actions or shy away from her accusations, he leaned in closer, catching every word between her sobs, patting her back softly and soothing her with his calm words.* Her impressions fluctuate radically. *I noticed my heart start to harden a bit toward the mother—perhaps it was she who couldn't be patient, flexible or more loving and tender toward her husband, who was a caring father!* Such interior monologues mimic Leslie's struggles to understand who her parents are and how to reconcile her role in relation to each one of them. She does not know how to hold both of them both close without distancing the other. Indeed, *Leslie felt anxious and nauseated, torn between her alliance with her mother against her father and her fear that she was betraying the father she once adored.*

Peter Blos (1976) notes that "adolescents have the tendency to see people and the world in 'black or white' . . . opposites remain, for the time being, irreconcilable, segmented, and absolute" (12). Leslie's world, no longer black and white, is full of questions she does not have the capacity to address; for example, how can she love and hate the same parent at the same time or embrace the fact that no one is completely bad or completely good? How does she transition from viewing her parents as a unit to seeing them as separate and separated people? How does she manage the internal turmoil of blaming her father, then her mother, then herself?

In an effort to understand her young patient's dilemma, Leslie's therapist tried to see it through the young girl's eyes—*to identify who was Good and who was Bad*—mirroring Leslie's own urge to assign blame as she struggles to absorb and accept that her life has changed and will be different now that her parents have split up. *Like Leslie, I felt as though forging an alliance with one meant loosening my grip on the other. Yet Leslie required the attention of both of her parents.*

She needed her parents to put her first, to protect her from their turmoil, and reestablish clear boundaries between them and her.

During the family crisis and the deterioration of their marriage, Leslie's parents were unable to protect her. However, despite the chaos of her parents' relationship, Leslie seeks to right herself and her world. With the invitation to her father to attend her therapy session, we sense Leslie's determination to return to the psychological work of adolescence, "the second individuation process" (Blos 1967, 162), even though it had been thrown off track. With the help of her father and her therapist, Leslie was able to sit quietly with her father, gripping his hand—on the road, perhaps, to reparation and growth.

IO SOLID STATE

My sixteen-year-old daughter, Naomi, and I enter the dining room of the assisted-living facility where my mother has lived for the past three years. I brace myself for the odor that I always associate with this place. Despite the fresh flowers and the potpourri scattered in bowls throughout the room, I still detect it, and every time I bend over my mother's snowy, rumpled hair to plant a kiss on her forehead, it is there: the smell of old age.

My eyes scan the room. I spot my mother at her usual table in the far corner, but her back is to us, and she does not yet know we're here. As we approach, one of her usual dinner companions, Sylvia, breaks into a broad smile and waves a gnarled hand at us.

"It's so wonderful you've come to see us again!" she gushes, in a tremulous voice. My mother turns her moon-shaped face to us and breaks into a big smile. "Hell-oo!" she says, drawing the word into two long syllables. Pleasure and affection wash over her features, and she inclines her head for our kisses.

My mother is eating her soup with a napkin tucked under her chin at one end. The other end is tucked under her half-empty bowl, creating a bridge to catch the stray bits of noodles and carrots that have fallen from her spoon. In addition to Sylvia, there is a third woman at the table, someone I haven't met before. She is relatively young, not more than sixty-five or sixty-six, and well put together. At first, I'm not sure if she is a visitor or resident, but after a few minutes, it is obvious that she is a resident, newly arrived. She reaches across the table to shake hands with us, politely asking if we've come here before. She wonders aloud if we like it here. We must, she decides, since we've returned. She looks over at Sylvia. "You must like it here, too, if you've come back," she reasons. Sylvia's wrinkled face breaks into a smile.

"Well, I can't come back if I've never left, now can I?" she remarks. "I've been here now for, let's see, maybe ten years? I've never left."

"So you like it," the other woman insists.

"Yes, I suppose," Sylvia sighs, "but I'm getting so old, so forgetful. It's a terrible thing, to lose your memories, it's just so—" she breaks off, frowning.

"It's frustrating, I think," I say to her.

"Yes, that's it!" she exclaims. "So frustrating."

Sylvia is one of my favorite residents here. She is either ninety-seven or 102—she isn't sure. But she does remember that she went to Wellesley College ("now that was a long time ago," she'll say), and she remembers that she used to go out dancing, wearing white gloves and staying out all night with "her gentleman friend." On a previous visit, she told me that right after graduation she traipsed to every shop in town, determined to get a job. She was hired at Macy's department store, where she advanced to sales manager. "I always wanted to work," she said with pride, "but it wasn't so easy for women back in those days . . ."

Abruptly, the new resident leans across the table toward my daughter. "Are you a scientist?" she inquires in a kind tone.

"No," Naomi says, "I'm in high school."

"She's getting ready for college," I add.

"Oh, college," says the woman, bobbing her head like a crane. "Are you a scientist?" she asks me.

"No, I'm a psychologist," I say.

"Oh, a psychologist, I see. Is your husband a scientist?"

"No, no, he's not." I reply. "Is your husband a scientist?"

It was the right question. She nods emphatically. "Yes, he is. A scientist. Solid state."

Sylvia adds helpfully, "Well, now we know everything."

We are visiting the facility a few days before Valentine's Day, and we have brought my mother cookies wrapped with a red bow. "What is this for?" she asks us. There are decorations strewn all over the dining room: red hearts on the table, streamers along the ceiling, pink hearts on the paper napkins.

"Can you guess?" Naomi asks her. My mother turns her head slowly toward Naomi, but just a bit beyond, as if the sound she has heard has come from somewhere behind Naomi's ear. She smiles bashfully and shakes her head no.

"But you can tell me, can't you?" she says to Naomi.

Naomi likes to encourage her. At sixteen, she is full of hope and magic, and she believes in the power of persistence. She tells her grandmother that yes, of course she'll tell her, but maybe they could try to guess together. All the hearts? The streamers? What could they mean? She wills her grandmother to take a guess, but her Nana just looks at her blankly.

Naomi gently and patiently takes my mother through the month, the date, and looks around for something, anything that might jog her memory. My mother is compliant enough but can muster no energy for the game. Finally, the new resident breaks in.

"I know what!" she exclaims. "Try December 25! You might know that one!"

My mother does know that date; she draws herself up a bit and inclines her head slowly toward the woman. "Well, you see, I'm Jewish, so it wouldn't matter, would it?" she asks gently. How would my mother—my pre-dementia mother, my Holocaust-survivor mother, my proper mother—feel if she knew that Christmas was in fact the only date she could still identify? A date that she recognized only as a day to discount, a day that was not, nor would ever be, hers? But I can see that the irony is lost on her.

"I just thought you might remember that one," the other woman says a bit defensively.

I remind my mother that the day before, December 24, has a special meaning to her. "It's your anniversary, remember?" I say.

At that, my mother's face brightens. "Oh, yes, I remember that," she says. "Your Daddy. Long time ago." Again, she turns her head slowly, searching for something I cannot discern. Her gaze lands on my daughter and rests there, expectantly. Naomi grows uncomfortable. She does not know how to interpret the empty space that hangs in the air between them, and for the moment, neither do I.

But this exchange seems to have agitated the new resident, and she starts to make a commotion. "Solid state, solid state, did you know?" she repeats. "Are you a scientist? Do you come here often? It's very nice. Is it solid state?"

My mother looks at me and lifts an eyebrow. *I may have lost my memory*, she seems to be saying to me, *but this one is off her rocker.* I am amused. I suddenly remember my father's old joke. "It's rude," he used to say, tongue-in-cheek, "to wag your finger like this [circling his index finger at his temple] when someone's nuts. Look, wag your finger down here [pointing to his chin] and say in Yiddish, 'ten centimeters up from here.'" That way, no one will know you're talking about them." It was an absurd joke, but it got me laughing every time. So I lean over to my mother and whisper the words in her ear: "*Zen s'ntym't'r.*" Recognition floods into her eyes, and she starts to laugh. Like a little girl, her giggles overcome her. For an alarming minute, she can't seem to stop, and I worry that she will choke or faint. But she does neither. And like a little girl, her giggles soon turn to soft hiccups. Then she is quiet.

Now the new resident breaks in to announce that she has lost her purse. It is nowhere to be seen. My mother looks down and lifts her soup spoon to her lips. The memory we shared has vanished. The light in her eyes has dimmed.

Analysts Reflection on the Aging Parent

> Beyond all the barriers,
> In the warm natural light
> Of simple day.
> I am allowed to give you
> Unstrained, flowing,
> Wise-infant
> To wise-mother love
>   —May Sarton (1978)

In the developmental arc, we are raised and parented, we grow to raise our own children, and then we take care of our aging parents. These phases of life and dependence contribute to a kaleidoscope that spans both intimacy and loss. In this chapter's vignette, we are introduced to our author, sandwiched between two generations, toggling among her roles as mother, as daughter, and as parent to her mother, who lives in an assisted-living facility. Our author prepares herself to face again the reality of her mother's decline and where she now lives. *I brace myself for the odor I always associate with this place . . . the smell of old age.* Her role, the role of parenting an aging parent, is difficult to bear. For this visit, she is buoyed by her teenage daughter, whose presence buttresses our author's sadness by keeping her role as mother-to-her-child in the foreground. The author relies on her daughter to express her own wish that her mother's mind be as agile as it once was. *She tells her grandmother that yes, of course she'll tell her, but maybe they could try to guess together.* It is likely that Naomi's gentle manner of encouraging her grandmother reflects the way her mother approached her developing mind as a young child.

Parents provide language for a young child's experience. By naming emotions, children come to know and recognize their own internal experiences (M. Balint 1968). In this way, parents help their children create a narrative of their lives. Here we see the reversal of this process: The author listens to Sylvia's story and offers the word that Sylvia was searching for to complete the thought and narrative. *"It's frustrating, I think," I say to her.* This story is replete with examples of trying to make connections where connections are lost. Naomi *gently and patiently* guides her grandmother, searching for *anything that might jog her memory* to weave a narrative.

Sandra Buechler (2012) tells us that losses that are unnamed are more difficult to mourn. In this story, we see our author use language to identify and integrate the gradual loss of her mother. In a poignant moment, when another resident asks her mother to recall the holiday that falls on December 25, our writer is confronted by the irony of her mother's memory of this (unhappy-for-her) date when she had lost the memory of so many happy ones.

So, what are the early roots that allow us to manage these shifts in our roles? As children, it is important that we know we can receive love without being annihilated and to give love without it being destructive (Fairbairn 1940, 1941). A child's loving gestures must be accepted by the parent in order to consolidate the critical feeling that one's love is good (Klein [1937] 1975; Fairbairn 1941; Searles 1975). Donald Winnicott (1954–1955, [1963a] 1965) notes that a nursing infant can feel he is depleting the mother, leading to guilt if there is no opportunity for reparation. Linda Kanefield (1985) writes:

> For the child to make reparation for this "depletion," an adult must be present to receive and accept the infant's love. The baby's anxiety . . . is a reaction to consuming and losing the mother, and it is tolerated and modified only by the confidence that the child can meaningfully contribute to the mother. It is this developmental

achievement that subsequently permits a more liberated risk-taking in the expression of instincts, and thereby fosters growth and maturity.

(14)

Indeed, the child's caretaking is interwoven with early strivings to create a healthy and psychologically intact mother who can provide "good enough mothering" (Winnicott [1953] 1958). If the mother is fragile, and if the child's attempts fail to shore her up through expressions of love, a child will postpone her own development in order to symbiotically function in a parental way (Searles 1975). The phrase "parentified child" captures this problematic role reversal.

In a healthy development, however, the parent's acceptance of a child's loving gestures contributes to the child's capacity to feel and demonstrate concern for another. In our story, we see the author's capacity to feel compassion and love for her diminished mother, and we see that her mother is still able to receive it. When her daughter and granddaughter greet her, *pleasure and affection wash over her features, and she inclines her head for our kisses.* Ultimately, these reverberating strengths enable an adult child to meaningfully care for an aging parent, successfully traveling "that developmental stage in which a child becomes the parent's parent" (Adelson 2000), to reinforce their parent-child bond. At the same time, this reversal of caretaking signals the impending loss of a parent and the recognition that childhood (being loved by a parent) is soon to be lost forever.

In this vignette we see the depth of the daughter's concern and her grief at no longer being a child. Our author's reminder of her parents' wedding anniversary date supplies the link to her mother's affective experience. The daughter holds what her mother can no longer access on her own, a meaningful vestige of their lives as a family unit. In that intimate moment, we sense that our storyteller is no longer the child, no longer held by a mother who tells and retells the narrative of her child's life. Adult children establish and secure a connection to the past for an aging parent, carrying a memory of how things used to be. For most of our lives, our relationships, creative ventures, and work are the sources of our self-esteem. With the isolation of old age, self-esteem is sustained primarily through feelings of being loved (Formanek 1986). When our author offers her mother the date of her anniversary without anger and without shaming her, her mother feels known and cherished.

Although psychoanalytic writers have paid far more attention to early development than to the later stages of life, we know that emotional challenges in adult life can revive earlier conflicts and latent family dynamics. In healthy relationships, the seeds of love and support sown in one's childhood will contribute to the readiness of an adult child to take on a caretaking or parental role to his or her parents. This new role offers the possibility of growth for the adult child and allows for the integration of new resolutions to old conflicts or disappointments. Mary-Joan Gerson (2018) describes the unanticipated "liberation" she felt in caring for her aging mother, finally feeling that she saw herself reflected back in her mother's eyes as the caring, loving, "wished-for daughter."

We notice how the world has shrunk for the aging adults in our story and how time unfolds at a slower pace. A new resident asks *Are you a scientist?* over and over, searching for a way back to the memory that it was her own husband who was a scientist. Leslye Russell (2015) writes:

> Perhaps it is this very shrinkage of the larger world that forces the psyche back upon the sensorium as a source of experience and meaning. The concreteness of the child, now present in old age, is the basis for something new; it is a return, a regression, and yet not a repetition. The old may be forced to slow down and their slowness is a sign of loss and impending death, but it is also exactly the right pace for beholding the beauty of the world.
>
> (83)

The small moments and strong connections portrayed in this vignette bring the solidity of the mother-child bond into focus.

Writing about losing patients when psychotherapies end, Sandra Buechler (2012) offers ideas that enrich our understanding of the dynamics we are witnessing here. Our author sustains a relationship with her mother with "grace . . . [forming a] decent memory, for myself and for her" (133). Their interaction generates a valuable memory for the author to cherish, even after her mother is gone. For the three generations in this story, memories rediscovered and shared contribute to the narrative of their relationships to each other, which will make loss more bearable.

The profound sorrow as one loses a mother through aging and dementia is accompanied by the loss of childhood. "Whatever loving care we have or have not received when we were not yet fully formed and still brimming with promise, there comes a time when childhood's opportunities end, or, at least, it seems to most like they should end" (Buechler 2012, 170). This stratified loss—the loss of the mother who was the caretaker, the loss of childhood, and the loss of who the author was in relation to her mother—permeates this story.

When our author, sensitively attuned to her mother's raised eyebrow, recalls an amusing Yiddish commentary shared by her family, she offers the link of memory to her mother. It is a gift that honors the loving family bonds her mother put in place, which has emboldened the author to take a parental role with her mother. *So I lean over to my mother and whisper the words in her ear: "Zen s'ntym't'r." Recognition floods into her eyes, and she starts to laugh. Like a little girl, her giggles overcome her.*

Sandra Buechler (2012) writes, "Only love gives us the courage it takes to cover the vast distances between our first and our last steps" (176).

PART THREE
Therapeutic Listening

II LOST CAT

It was four weeks after my father's bicycle accident that he awoke from a coma.

At the time, I was just twenty-three years old, and I hadn't fully grasped how devastated I was. Each day I would picture him either flying over his handlebars or on a breathing tube, and each night I dreamt that he was speaking to me, reassuring me that he was fine, that it wasn't nearly as serious as everyone thought, and that he wanted me to get him back home.

Of course, he wasn't fine. We soon learned that he would never recover from the massive brain damage that would impair his mobility, eradicate his speech entirely, and render him completely dependent on others.

For weeks after the diagnosis, I'd wake up in tears. I didn't want my boyfriend to touch or comfort me. I felt numb and as cold as stone. When an older friend suggested that I go into therapy, I stared at her, bewildered. It had never occurred to me to "see someone," although I had been considering getting a degree in clinical psychology. After more persuading, I scheduled an appointment.

I cannot remember a single thing I said during that first session; all I recall is that I talked for the entire session, nonstop, never giving the therapist a chance to say a word. He looked kind, however, and I really didn't care whether he spoke or not. I discovered, to my amazement, that I had a lot to say. For the first time since my father's accident, I felt at peace, even liberated. I readily agreed to return the following week.

One day before my second meeting with the therapist, my boy-friend called to tell me that he had lost my cat. He had agreed to take my cat to the vet while I was at work, and instead of taking him in the car, he placed the cat in the saddlebag at the rear of his bike. He didn't feel right closing the bag all the way, so he had left it partially open. At a busy intersection, the terrified cat jumped out of the bag and disappeared.

As he told me what happened, I grew more and more furious, unable to stop replaying the scene in my mind, of my trembling cat dashing through busy traffic. He kept apologizing, and I yelled at him, "How could you do that? What were you thinking? Why did you have to ride your stupid bike?" By the time I entered the parking garage of my therapist's building that afternoon, I despaired of ever finding my cat again. I collapsed into his reclining chair and started sobbing. Bit by bit I related the story of my rage and grief over losing my cat. The therapist listened in sympathetic silence, murmuring a mild "mmm hmm" now and then, and offered me a box of Kleenex. I spent this second session talking about my cat—the first pet I'd ever had—who was doglike in his devotion and would follow me around the house, carrying my smelly gym socks in his mouth. It seemed I couldn't bear another loss.

Finally finished with my outpouring, I sat hunched in the chair, spent. For the first time, there was silence in the room. I awaited his wise and comforting words. Looking at me with large sad eyes, he cleared his throat and said, "Cats are such sensitive critters, aren't they?"

I froze. Suddenly I thought of Max, the boy I had a crush on in the fifth grade. The crush abruptly ended when I watched him being bullied on the bus, and once off the bus, when he was no longer in danger, he stuck his tongue out at his adversary. He looked pathetic. I had to look away, unsure if I was protecting him or me.

I picked up my tissues, walked out my therapist's door, and never returned.

Analysts Reflect on Need for Attunement

> People only ask questions when they're ready to hear the answers.
> —John Irving, *The Cider House Rules*

The shock of learning that a parent has been tragically impaired by a bicycle accident is deeply and emotionally disruptive, particularly for a young adult who has had no reason to consider her father's vulnerability or mortality. For weeks, the young woman in the story is suspended between daytime—*images of him either flying over his handlebars or on a breathing tube*—and the escape into her nightly dreams—*that he was speaking to me, reassuring me that he was just fine, that it wasn't nearly as serious as everyone thought*—only to be traumatized by the reality of his condition upon wakening. She rejects her boyfriend's efforts to comfort her, not wanting or able to feel. Numbness provided some psychic distance, and bewildered, she seeks to simultaneously absorb yet not absorb her father's condition.

Like many of our patients, this woman finds her way to a therapist's office, guided by a friend's recommendation that she needs to express and integrate her pain. Eric Mendelsohn (2018) illuminates the powerful "poetics and pragmatics" of first meetings in treatment, articulating the need for resonance of communication to establish the tone for co-creating a healing relationship. While easy to overlook, this first encounter portends what is to come. To her surprise, the young woman in this chapter's vignette has a lot to tell the kind-looking therapist, and he does not interfere with the flow of her words. When she leaves the first session, she *felt at peace, even liberated*. The nascent therapeutic engagement is positive. She schedules a second session.

Freud ([1913] 1963) notes, "The first aim of the treatment consists in attaching [the patient] to the treatment and to the person of the physician" (152). Without some sliver of relief or optimism, it is difficult for a patient to begin to make this attachment. Freud continues, "To ensure this, one need do nothing but allow [the patient] time. . . . It is certainly possible to forfeit . . . success if from the start one takes up any standpoint other than one of sympathetic understanding" (152). Jane Hall (1988) puts it succinctly, "The main goal of the first meeting . . . is to have more meetings" (64). Recognizing the strength required for a distraught patient to make the initial contact, Hall emphasizes that a warm, safe atmosphere is essential for deepening the treatment. The ambiance of the therapeutic space is meant to build trust in the therapist and to enable the patient to begin to heal.

Carrying the hope for healing into her second session, the young woman sobs, telling her therapist how she is reeling from losing her beloved cat and enraged at her boyfriend, who had lost him.

While we need not be trained as psychotherapists to register the affectively raw connections between this young woman's two sessions, analysts seek to respond in a way that conveys our efforts to understand. We must choose carefully what to say or not to say so that our caring and helpful presence is conveyed to a patient swirling in pain. Our young woman recalls her therapist's *mild "mmm hmm"* and his offer of tissues, which prompted more details about her strong bond with her cat.

Kyle Arnold (2012) explores the many meanings of the "mm-hmm" murmurings of an analyst. In this story, the analyst's sympathetic sounds yield the space to the patient and what she strives to communicate while simultaneously indicating that he is right there along with her, encouraging a more elaborate telling. In the first session, he functions therapeutically as the "unobtrusive analyst" (Grossmark 2012), quietly joining his patient in co-creating the relational atmosphere she needs to contain and process unbearable events.

Arnold also explains that an analyst's sounds can serve to avoid difficult affect, including the patient's rage, by giving the appearance of being present while subtly withdrawing. This young woman's perception of her therapist as sympathetically attuned is disrupted when he finally speaks. *"Cats are such sensitive critters, aren't they?"* With that misattuned comment—a flat platitude—the young woman's hope for compassionate understanding and containment of her profound confusing rage vanishes. Perhaps her therapist suspected that she felt as lost and abandoned as her cat and was trying to speak to his new patient through that medium. Perhaps the therapist expected his comment would gently help his patient integrate the profound losses she was facing. But he missed—or avoided—what was most salient to this young woman: she was desperate to understand her inner turmoil and needed relief from the pounding storm of rage and sorrow inside. With the therapist's comment, she felt insufficiently held, let down, and alone.

Immediately she recalls a boy she had a crush on in childhood. That crush ended when she watched him being bullied, a mental association to his fall from grace and an end to the possibilities this childhood crush held for her. In psychoanalytic treatment, we rely on our patients' associations to inform us of their unconscious feelings in the moment. So what does our patient's seemingly unrelated yet specific memory tell us about her response to her new therapist and to the horrifying events that brought her to treatment? The patient realizes, once the therapist utters his atonal comment, that he is not the right person to help her. She associates him both with her father's current condition (vulnerable and weak) and with her boyfriend (careless and inept at comforting her). Without her sorrowful rage addressed and contained, she could not feel safe in this treatment.

Patients enter treatment in a vulnerable state. We can appreciate that the young woman in this chapter, facing the loss of her father as she has known him, the loss of family life as she has known it, and the loss of her companion cat would be catapulted from stability and security to terrifying helplessness.

Roy Schafer (1983) elucidates the components of the analytic attitude that promote therapeutic engagement and safety in the context of such terror. His formulations help us comprehend what went amiss in this therapist's early opportunities to create an alliance: this young woman comes to treatment, mobilizing hope in this new relationship yet also petrified that she will be let down once she exposes her pain. She needs her therapist to demonstrate his readiness to see and tolerate her "devastated" state of mind, and she seeks evidence that he can safeguard her capacity for an integrated self. Schafer writes, "Another aspect of the affirmative self is the analyst's . . . assuming coherence and potential intelligibility in everything the analysand brings up or refrains from bringing up. The analyst is prepared to see the analysand as a meaningful totality" (47). For this young woman, shattered by tragedy, it is particularly important for the analyst to convey her belief in her patient's coherence. She is "living in dread, continuously anticipating or experiencing actual or potential agonizing conflict and loss" (46). When the story's therapist offers an impersonal, superficial statement, it creates too large a gap between the terror of his patient's experience and his benign tone, however well meaning it might have been. He failed to hold the totality of her experience.

So how do we sense what a patient needs in treatment? A growing body of infant developmental research (Stern 1985; Beebe and Lachmann 2002, 2013) utilizing split-screen videotaping of moment-to-moment interactions in mother/infant dyads offers us some new insights. Emotional attunement between mothers and infants can be observed through "interpersonal communion" (Stern 1985, 146), in which the mother matches the intensity, intensity contour, temporal beat, rhythm, duration, and shape of an infant's affect state. Stern also identifies "nonpurposeful misattunement" (149), when "the mother incorrectly identified, to some extent, the quantity and/or quality of the infant's feeling state, or she was unable to find in herself the same internal state." While caregivers—and therapists—need not respond with perfect attunement at all times, our bereft patient has little resilience to tolerate any misattunement. Her therapist's words fall distressingly short of matching the intensity, contour, and duration of her cries. She is not comforted. She took a risk and feels abandoned yet again.

As to how we address a patient's need for more accurate attunement, Howard Bacal (1998) offers the concept of "optimal responsiveness," the necessary empathic accuracy needed to build therapeutic relatedness. He believes that understanding is the central curative aspect of treatment. The analyst's understanding "response must be commensurate with the patient's level of . . . [developmental] organization or degree of intactness" (18). Communication of the analyst's understanding is most meaningful when it is particular to a particular patient in that particular moment. In our story, the therapist initially meets his patient with attuned understanding, notably reducing her distress by the end of the first session. However, he fails to sustain this attunement in the second session. The young patient is desperate to reestablish her bearings in the context of overwhelming events and chaotic feelings. Her therapist's vague comment seems insipid by contrast. As Bacal warns, treatment can break down when the patient's "needs are greater than the analyst's capacity to understand and respond at a particular moment."

Winnicott ([1963d] 1965) provides another way to make sense of the aborted treatment in our story. As analysts, we nurture maturation by providing a stable, nourishing environment for the patient to adapt and grow, even in the face of trauma. Our shared familiarity with the vicissitudes of human experience facilitates the healing process. He writes:

> One can only assume that understanding in a deep way and interpreting at the right moment is a form of reliable adaptation. . . . In innumerable ways we meet our patient's needs because we know what the patient is feeling like, more or less, and we can find the

equivalent of the patient in ourselves. What we have in ourselves we can project, and find in the patient. All this is done silently, and the patient usually remains unaware of what we do well, but becomes aware of the part we play when things go wrong. It is when we fail in these respects that the patient reacts to the unpredictable and suffers a break in the continuity of his going-on-being.

(250)

In this chapter's story, the therapist's response is traumatizing for his patient, and she leaves treatment. We can read between the lines that the therapist is unable to find the patient's terror in himself and unable to impart his calming self so that he can locate that strength in his suffering patient. Perhaps the therapist believes he is making an empathic comment; his patient's response provides the evidence that he has not. She gathers herself and leaves, protecting herself from more searing pain, and, frightened that her therapist will not be able to tolerate her "tidal wave of rage," she protects him as well.

As analysts, we find it disconcerting when we feel we have connected with a patient but are met with an unexpected ending to our work together. We revisit such abrupt endings in our minds and with our colleagues, unsettled by our patient's decision to discontinue with us. We are saddened to read of this young woman who seeks help to cope with life-altering losses but leaves feeling angry and alone. At the same time, we glimpse this young woman's resourcefulness and inner strength: she leaves treatment when she is not sufficiently understood.

12 INTOXICATING POWER

Twenty-three and petite, Stephanie routinely arrived at her sessions wearing baggy sweatpants and collared shirts buttoned up to her neck. Her clothes, too large by a size or two, looked as if she had worn them to bed. Her long hair hung in front of her face like a curtain, hiding her from the world. At times she appeared so timid and waif-like that I felt the urge to reach out and offer her my hand.

Listening to Stephanie, I sensed her strong need for reassurance and encouragement. She reminded me of what it felt like to be the last girl picked in gym class, and I felt enormous compassion for her. Stephanie filled our early sessions with the myriad ways she felt badly about herself, as if to convince me that she lacked any valuable qualities. Yet I found her likable and engaging: she was intelligent and had a good sense of humor, and when I could see beyond the clothes and hair, I saw an appealing young woman.

She described her childhood with an unhappy and unfulfilled mother who resented giving up her career to take care of her children. Her mother's depression and denial of Stephanie's sexuality and attractiveness still resonated with her. And even though Stephanie secretly believed her father favored her over her older sister, she rarely interacted with him during her teen years, when he retreated from his nagging, depressed wife, leaving Stephanie to pick up the pieces.

Stephanie told me that she had no interest in dating. In fact, she fended off any attention from men. "No makeup, nothing revealing," was her goal. She worried that if she looked at all pleasing, she would be seen as "sleazy" or seductive. I could easily imagine her alone on a weekend night, sequestered and depriving herself of the social pleasures of other young adults.

In those first months, we explored her dramatically low self-esteem. I struggled to understand why she felt so undeserving. She would return to her list of deficiencies like it was a mantra: she was not smart enough, not interesting enough, not attractive enough. While I was tempted to contradict her, I refrained, because I knew that reassurance would likely offer no real relief or change. Even so, I would gently steer the conversation in a direction that would reveal her positive attributes. I kept thinking that if she could see her potential like I did, she could begin to build a more hopeful view of herself.

After a time, Stephanie's oft-repeated self-criticisms began to feel decidedly redundant and hollow. The sessions deadened. My empathic comments made little difference to her self-perception. As Stephanie persisted in presenting this narrow and negative view of herself, it gradually dawned on me that there was more to her story.

One afternoon, Stephanie arrived visibly upset. "I hate that Charles is paying so much attention to me. He's always trying to talk to me." She cried, her eyes downcast, her nose running. "It is so awful. I can't believe he flirted with me like that. Why would he even be interested in me?" she sniffled.

Suddenly, something in me shifted. I felt like I was watching a performance. "You know," I said, with a lifted eyebrow and a bit of a smile, "I'm not sure I believe you."

She looked up, her eyes wide for a second. "What do you . . .," and she stopped mid-sentence. Then she began to laugh, a deep hearty laugh, the first I had heard since her therapy began. Her face brightened, her shoulders relaxed. "You're right. It's not really how I feel at all. I actually love it! You know, it sort of feels better to admit it. I really do love the attention. I can't believe I'm telling you this."

After that exchange, our work started to shift. Stephanie revealed her secret fear that she had an "intoxicating power over men." She worried that if she "let herself go" and revealed her beauty, she would seduce men and cause destruction—like Helen of Troy. Instead, she chose to keep her body and its longings tightly under wraps.

Stephanie recognized that she was conflicted about drawing attention to herself. With friends, she would act demurely and self-effacing, but secretly she would flirt and try to capture a man's attention. We came to see that hiding her wish to be noticed was a way to protect herself from other women's envy and rejection. Only later did she confess to having envious and competitive feelings.

Gradually, Stephanie began to inhabit the space in my office more fully. She started to take pleasure in her wit, her intelligence, and her instinctive flair for fashion. I marveled at her transformation and the ways in which she had become both thoughtful and playful in our sessions. It was getting harder and harder to remember the insecure young woman who had arrived at my door just a year earlier.

Analysts Reflect on Expansion of Empathy

> Atticus was right. One time he said you never really know a man until you stand in his shoes and walk around in them.
> —Harper Lee, *To Kill a Mockingbird*

The self-effacing young woman in this story elicits warm, sympathetic feelings in her therapist: *She reminded me of what it felt like to be the last girl picked in gym class, and I felt enormous compassion for her.* Her therapist listens and is curious about why she has such low self-esteem, but notices that *after a time, Stephanie's oft-repeated self-criticisms began to feel decidedly redundant and hollow. The sessions deadened. My empathic comments made little difference to her self-perception.*

Our story's therapist observes that Stephanie might be presenting only a partial set of feelings when she claims to be upset about a young man's interest in her and says, *"You know . . . I'm not sure I believe you."* While this comment may sound confrontational, the laugh of recognition it produces confirms that it hit the mark. Rather than offending the patient, this clinical moment provides a pivotal juncture in the work and moves the treatment from emptiness to liveliness. This exchange offers us an expanded and complex view of empathy.

Empathy means "to feel oneself into the shape of another." (In German, the word is *einfuehlung*, which literally translates as "one feeling.") Colloquially, we "put ourselves in another's shoes" to enter their subjective experience. Empathy is critical to therapists' work in that it provides an inroad to our patients' feelings. It is both a tool to observe and understand their emotional experience and a characteristic of the rapport needed for change to occur (Ferenczi 1928; Schwaber 1981; Stone 1981; Wolf 1988; Lichtenberg 1981; Kohut et al. 1984; Abend 1986; Bolognini 2009). Neuroscientists have shown that there are "mirror neurons" that are stimulated at points of social contact (Gallese 2001). These neurons are activated when we are moved, for example, by fictional characters we relate to in a movie or book or by the stories our friends or patients tell us—even if we have not had a similar experience.

Building on Freud's ([1905] 1955) early notion that empathy is needed to understand another, Fliess (1942) describes empathy as a trial identification with the patient—a way we come to know another's experience by feeling some aspect of it within ourselves. Privileging the significance of empathy in treatment, Kohut ([1959] 1978) highlights the analyst's use of introspection and empathy to observe and communicate understanding within the therapeutic dyad. We view a patient's material through the process of "vicarious introspection," an empathic receptivity to recognize another's experience in oneself. Kohut (1977), in an oft-quoted passage, states the critical necessity of empathy:

> Man can no more survive psychologically in a psychological milieu that does not respond empathically to him than he can survive physically in an atmosphere that contains no oxygen. . . . The analyst's behavior vis-à-vis his patient should be the expected average one— i.e., the behavior of a psychologically perceptive person vis-à-vis someone who is suffering and has entrusted himself to him for help.
>
> (253)

In Stephanie's story, we hear the therapist's empathic resonance with her unhappy, lonely patient. *In those first months, we explored her dramatically low self-esteem. I struggled to understand why she felt so undeserving.* The therapist turns inward to her own reservoir of experience—as we do when we work—sensing more complexity than what Stephanie presents in the litany of failings she repeats again and again. The therapist's intuition is built on empathy, which includes the ability to step back and evaluate the experience. As Greenson (1960) conceives of it, "Empathy and intuition are related. Both are special methods of gaining quick and deep understanding. One empathizes to reach feelings; one uses intuition to get ideas. Empathy is to affects and impulses what intuition is to thinking. Empathy often leads to intuition" (422).

When Stephanie expresses distress that a young man flirts with her, her therapist observes her own internal shift and says, "*You know . . . I'm not sure I believe you.*" With this comment, the exploratory space opens up between patient and therapist. The therapist transforms what had been an intuitive feeling into a formulated thought that addressed what Stephanie had pushed to the side. Now Stephanie could begin to acknowledge those previously disavowed feelings.

How do we understand the impact of this shift in the context of empathy?

Consider the Ornsteins' (1985) notion of "the empathic vantage point": in their view, holding an empathic stance contributes to a patient "feeling understood *in depth* this time, rather than only in terms of the feeling states that arise in the moment-to-moment interchanges" (52). Deep empathic resonance requires more than being attuned to what a patient is aware of thinking and feeling—it must also include listening for what lies beyond the patient's awareness. Stephanie recognizes the truth in her therapist's observation when she responds, *"You're right. It's not really how I feel at all. I actually love it!"* The Ornsteins write: "Evidence for the progression and deepening of the analytic process is provided by the lessening of the patient's need for the defensive use of repression and disavowal. With this lessening, the split-off parts of the self will be increasingly experienced as part of the total, expanding, and now more unified self" (53). As therapists, we recognize that our patients ask us to recognize and safeguard their unacceptable feelings, whether they are aware of them or not.

We notice that this shift in the therapist comes at a moment when she senses that Stephanie, sufficiently bolstered by her therapist's understanding, can tolerate perceptions of herself that were previously unwelcome. As Bromberg (1998) writes, "Optimally, [the analyst] should try to be experientially accessible to the impact of those moments in which he becomes aware that a shift in self-state (either his own or the patients) has taken place" (279). Bromberg illuminates such a shift, saying,

> My conscious *awareness* of the shift in the intersubjective field, because it changes my mode of processing what is being heard . . . eventually becomes "usable" because I am no longer hearing the patient's words and my own in the context I was hearing them before the shift. I am now experiencing their meaning being shaped by the participation of another aspect of the patient's self that has been engaged with an aspect of my own self in enacting something beyond what the words had earlier appeared to be conveying.
>
> (279)

The therapist observes that *after that exchange, our work started to shift*. Although Stephanie was initially reluctant to acknowledge the seductive, competitive, and powerful aspects of her femininity, she could now claim those feelings and the conflicts they engender. Her therapist's capacity to hold all of Stephanie's self-states in mind facilitates her emerging ability to inhabit those parts of herself.

Bromberg (1998) helps us make sense of these previously disavowed self-perceptions that gradually become more integrated for Stephanie as her therapy progresses. Treatment, he writes, "allows a patient's here-and-now perception of self to share consciousness with the experiences of incompatible self-narratives that were formerly dissociated" (278). This capacity to tolerate the "multiplicity of self" (272) is not only normal but essential to having a cohesive sense of self over time. We all have ordinary states of consciousness that are shifting and discontinuous. As Howell (2005) reports, "Research in cognitive psychology, neurophysiology, and child development indicates that the brain, the mind, and the self are normally multiple and that the idea of the unity of the self is an illusion" (39).

The therapeutic evolution in Stephanie's story reflects considerable growth through therapy. As Bromberg writes:

Health is the ability to stand in the spaces between realities without losing any of them—the capacity to feel like one self while being many. "Standing in the spaces" is a shorthand way of describing a person's capacity to make room at any given moment for subjective reality that is not readily containable by the self he experiences as "me" at that moment.

(274)

As we reflect on the therapist's empathy, we observe that she sees in Stephanie what Stephanie cannot see in herself—nor could her depressed and envious mother: *I found her likable and engaging: she was intelligent and had a good sense of humor, and when I could see beyond the clothes and hair, I saw an appealing young woman.* Our patients come to treatment with areas of thwarted development accompanied by the often-overlooked "forward edge" healthy strivings. As analysts, we attend to the "forward edge tendrils" (Tolpin 2002). We try to hold in mind our patients' potential, thereby creating the space for them to discover who they will become.

Our story's therapist empathically resonates with those aspects of Stephanie that were insufficiently nurtured. As she listens, she hears that Stephanie is yearning to have her flirtatious, powerful, sexual, feminine aspects of herself revived and accepted. Although the early treatment is characterized by a repetition of "the trailing edge" (181), we recognize her therapist's capacity to see her as much more. The therapist wants to help Stephanie take pleasure in aspects of herself that her depressed, envious mother could not.

Empathically attuned verbal responsiveness fosters the integration of disparate affective experiences, and it contributes to the resumption of development, the softening of self-sabotaging perceptions, and the tolerance of conflict and uncomfortable feelings. Stephanie's therapist facilitates this transformation, and as their work hits the one-year mark, she realizes, *It was getting harder and harder to remember the insecure young woman who had arrived at my door just a year earlier.*

13 STEPPING OVER THE THRESHOLD

One morning at 11 a.m., I walk out to greet a new patient, Sophie, only to find the waiting room of my home office empty. Assuming that she is running late, I return to my consulting room to wait. After a few minutes, I hear a loud knock at the front door of my house, some two hundred feet away from my office entrance. Might this be my new patient? In my phone conversation with Sophie, I was careful to explain how to get to my office, which is well marked and easy to find. Rarely do patients have trouble locating it.

Sophie is the exception. I run down my office stairs, across the house, and open my front door. I greet Sophie and gently explain that my office door is to the right of the house. Stepping outside to point her in the right direction, I let her know that I will meet her there. I walk through the house to return to my office and await her arrival—still no Sophie. Puzzled, I walk outside to see where she is. That's when I hear banging coming from somewhere far off. I follow the sound to the back of my house, where Sophie is knocking on the patio door. This time I escort her to my office door, a door that she passed moments earlier on her way to the backyard.

Sitting with Sophie at our first meeting, I had many (internal) questions about her entrance and confusion: What does this all mean? Why couldn't Sophie find the way in? But I say nothing about the directional mishaps; I simply acknowledge that it has been an ordeal. I understand that neither of us can know yet what this moment means, so I wait.

Several sessions later, Sophie begins by saying, "I hate walking into the lounge at work. When I went there today, several people were sitting together talking. I felt like an alien."

"An alien?" I ask.

"An alien," she answered, enunciating the word. "You know it's funny, but I remember being a kid on the playground. I always wanted to join in with the other girls who were playing, but I never knew how. I'd either stand back or barge in awkwardly. I could never find the right way in. The more nervous I was, the clumsier I would be. So instead, I just went off by myself. In my head I would play this game, where I pretend I am an alien from Mars and that I had landed on Earth to observe these humans." She continued, "I would act like I didn't care, or that I didn't want to play. But really I had no idea how to make a connection." She went on to describe her loneliness, despair, and isolation.

I paused before responding. "The way you talk about trying to make friends but not knowing how to find your way in, and feeling like an alien, reminds me of our first meeting when you couldn't find your way in to see me."

Sophie began to cry. After a few moments, she said, "That's exactly right. I was so anxious coming here that day. I can't even tell you how bad it was, I couldn't think straight. It was so awful. I felt so crazy. Even when you showed me the side door, I was confused . . . you probably thought I *was* some kind of alien." She laughs.

I invite her to tell me more about these aliens.

She paused and then responds, "*ET* . . . the movie *ET* just popped into my head." She shares more about her childhood fantasy that there is another home, far away, that she can return to and feel safe. That was the moment when Sophie opened the door, stepped over the threshold, and our journey together began.

Analysts Reflect on Timing and Tact

> Somewhere we know that without silence words lose their meaning, that without listening speaking no longer heals, that without distance closeness cannot cure.
>
> —Henri Nouwen

As therapists, we naturally wonder why Sophie couldn't find her way into her therapist's office and what her panic might mean. We know from training and experience that it is important to sit patiently with our questions so that they can be answered by Sophie in her own words and in her own time. Like all of our patients, Sophie needed to feel safe, heard, and understood before she could do the hard work of therapy.

Doing our job well as therapists requires that we allow our interactions with patients and our understanding of them to unfold without preconceptions. Our work is to wait, to listen to the voices within ourselves, and discover what the patient has hidden and needs to reveal. If our timing and tact are off and we leap too quickly to nail down the meaning of an exchange, we flatten the story, flatten the experience of our patient, and flatten our capacity to understand and treat him or her.

How do we help our patients reveal their stories? We do this first by listening. We avoid formulaic explanations and relying on theory. A theory, like a story, is a way of seeing and understanding the world—sometimes it can lead to a deep-seated truth, and at other times it can lead us off course. When we hear a patient's history and decide, "oh, yes, clearly this explains that . . . or . . . that," we rob the individual and the treatment of its richness, complexity, and meaning. While we rely on theories to inform our thinking, once in the consulting room, we need to put them aside and instead invite our patients' curiosity and their own exploration of their inner landscape. Collaboratively, we search for ways to connect more deeply with their experience—instead of prematurely imposing our view of their terrain.

There are multiple truths to unravel in any clinical material and many ways to look at it. As with the Indian parable of the blind men and the elephant, no matter how true or accurate one's subjective experience may be, seeing how all the pieces fit together is essential and takes time. One blind man might feel the elephant's leg, for example, and assume he's touching a tree trunk.

Like these blind men, we analysts all have our templates for perceiving and listening to our patients, but templates alone are too simple and not enough. Instead, we work toward a richness of language and meaning by gathering up our patients' bits and pieces of memories, fantasies, associations, pains, passions, and dreams. As with a great sentence, the language of an apt interpretation must be formed in a way that will touch or resonate with the other. Without a meaningful experience in the moment or a story to accompany the feeling, there is no real contact, no emotional depth (Stern 2004). Meaningful psychological change requires that both patient and therapist remain open to unplanned and unpredictable moments, which can transport us to places we never expected when the treatment began (Hoffman 1998; Slavin and Kriegman 1998). There is a thrill to these untrodden paths and where they can lead us.

Sophie comes to see her therapist seeking relief from dysthymia—a lifelong, chronic sadness. She needs her story to emerge slowly and without any urgency or pressure to reach a resolution. What if her therapist had said to Sophie in that first meeting, "Why do you think you had trouble finding my door?" or "What were you feeling when you couldn't find my door?" She may have answered, "I was anxious." Or she might have felt defensive and said, "I don't know why. I just couldn't find the right door." Or worse yet, in her distress, she may have felt ashamed and decided not to return, precluding any opportunity for us to become collaborators or cowriters on a shared journey.

In these imagined exchanges between Sophie and her therapist, there is no moment of surprise or true engagement. We don't learn anything new about Sophie, nor do we gain access to any deep connection to what had occurred that day. Rather than bringing us in closer contact, it may only have made our work more difficult. And even if the therapist had correctly understood and interpreted the meaning of Sophie's difficulty finding her way in, the timing would have been insensitive at best.

In this first meeting with her new therapist, Sophie could not yet have felt safe enough to link ideas to make meaning or to experience what Donald Winnicott called a "holding" environment (Winnicott 1965),[1] an "environment, [that] when good-enough, facilitates the maturational process" ([1963c] 1965), 223, 239) of the infant. Winnicott clarifies that the facilitating environment does not enable the infant to grow or determine the direction of its growth but instead adapts itself to the changing needs of the maturing infant.

A similar process takes place in a "good-enough" therapy. A safe, holding, facilitating environment is established by the therapist, which nurtures the patient's development. Creating an atmosphere of safety takes time.

Sophie's therapist patiently listens. Sophie brings her ongoing feelings of being an outsider into the session. She relates them to painful childhood memories of feeling like an "alien" when she wanted desperately to belong to a group of other children but didn't know how to join in. Here is a moment of meaning for this therapeutic pair, where they can discover something previously unformed and turn it into something that they can explore together. For Sophie, the image of an "alien" crystallizes her experience and provides a bridge, helping her express what has been out of reach, bringing her story to life. And for the therapist, she can now join Sophie on that bridge so that they can walk it together.

14 UGLY SHOES

Rosa hesitantly approaches my open door, peering in, as if waiting for an invitation. As usual, she is dressed in all gray and black, seeming to blend in to the background, despite the wild curly hair that surrounds her petite face. For a moment, I am surprised by my cruel urge to make her wait. Instead, I nod encouragement for her to enter.

On tiptoes Rosa crosses the room, slouching like a schoolgirl trying to avoid notice. She pauses, then whispers, "I'm so sorry." With elaborate care, Rosa removes her shoes, signaling, "I wouldn't dream of dirtying your couch." In the waiting room, Rosa had overheard the patient before her give a loud, raucous laugh. "You've never laughed like that with me," she remarks sadly as she lies back on the couch.

As I begin to reply, her body tenses, on alert for what I might say. "Perhaps you felt hurt and couldn't help but be curious about what was going on," I venture.

"No, I'm sure everyone is different . . . it's just that I thought, 'You must be having fun in here.' I don't know if you ever feel that way with me."

Once again, I feel frustrated, silently accused. Is there nothing I could say that wouldn't wound her?

I recall the day she wept on the couch, telling me of the car accident when she was five years old. Her father had swerved to avoid a truck and crashed into a tree. In the ambulance, terrified, Rosa heard a shrieking voice and realized it was her own. Twenty-five years later, I can barely see the scar on her right cheek. But for her, the scar continues to blaze bright red.

Today, I look at her lying on the couch and find myself staring at the shoes she has meticulously lined up on the floor: black, scuffed, lace-up shoes with no style. Rosa, who spent most days running after her toddler, probably thought little of her footwear; a sturdy, comfortable shoe was what she required. But for some reason, their clunkiness irritated me. The shoes seemed to declare: because of my scar, I am destined to be Plain Jane, never pretty, never put together. I think to myself with a silent chuckle, I'll know she is ready to end analysis when she stops wearing such ugly shoes! That thought is immediately followed by another: how ridiculous, I had shoes almost just like hers.

With a sigh, Rosa tells me about going to the opera with her mother-in-law. There they ran into her mother-in-law's friend, who recently had a facelift. As they took their seats, Rosa's mother-in-law leaned toward her and hissed, "No matter the surgery, her face will never be perfect. She is just too homely." Beginning to cry and pointing to her scar, Rosa said, "I don't understand how she could say that in front of me."

Rosa often talked about her scar, the world a mirror, reflecting back a distorted version of herself—ugly and damaged. "I remember being in the emergency room after the car accident. After that, I never looked the same." Rosa reaches for a tissue. "They wouldn't even let my mother go to surgery with me!" Wiping her nose, she continues, "They wrenched me away from her and strapped me to the table. The nurse told me to stop crying. She said that if I kept crying my face would look ugly forever, and the doctor wouldn't be able to fix it. I was five years old!" She takes a breath.

"It must have been frightening to be there alone," I say. "And there must have been a lot of pain as well, both during and then after, while you were recovering."

Rosa seems startled. "There was, I guess," she says. "It's strange; I don't think I've ever thought about what it felt like." She pauses. "But I do remember wailing and squirming away while my mother held a cold compress to my face. I was swollen for weeks after. She would hold the compress to my cheek, and she would just cry and cry, leaning over me, trying to get me to keep still. All the while I kicked and pushed her hands away."

As Rosa spoke, a memory began to tug at the edge of my awareness. Suddenly I see a thrashing, screaming toddler lying on her back in her crib. That toddler is me. My mother stands over me, helplessly crying. She is trying to jam my misshapen feet, curved inward like boomerangs (the effects of metatarsus adductus) into stiff leather shoes. The shoes were attached by a perpendicular steel bar; the bar swiveled when I walked, forcing my feet apart to shift and straighten my malformed bones. How I hated those shoes!

I'd thrash and flail around, making it nearly impossible for my mother to put them on my feet. Not only were the shoes painful to wear, but they prevented me from running and jumping. Angrily, I'd storm through our apartment. The man in the apartment below us would bang on the ceiling with a broom, yelling, "Stop all that racket up there! Can't you shut that kid up?!" Mornings and evenings, my mother would also put me through a rigorous, painful exercise regimen; I resisted that too. For years, long after the corrective shoes with a bar had been put away, I had to wear ugly, uncomfortable, lace-up orthopedic shoes with special inserts to strengthen my bones. I never got to wear loafers—the ones with a shiny new penny tucked in the slot—that I longed for, the ones all my friends wore.

Now, sitting with Rosa, my irritation suddenly dropped away, and in its place I felt compassion for the suffering she had endured and the scar she could not erase. An old reservoir of pain had opened up inside of me, and I saw clearly what she had been trying to tell me—and why I could not hear her. My childhood shame about my body and its deformities had resonated with her pain outside of my awareness. Instead of empathizing with her, my mind had pushed away my shameful memory and, with it, Rosa's pain.

With that insight, I was able to respond more directly, more fully, even playfully. Now she no longer paused in the doorway but seemed to look forward to the sessions, and a new warmth and shared sense of humor emerged. Together we discovered she had a wry wit and a ready laugh. As things progressed, I also noticed that Rosa had begun to dress more attractively. One day, she flew into my office a little breathless, carrying a shopping bag from Saks Fifth Avenue. Laughing sheepishly, she said, "I'm sorry I am so late, the saleswoman was so distracted! But look what I got—I just couldn't resist." She pulled out a shoebox and lifted the lid. Inside was a pair of patent leather pumps with a delicate checkered bow on top. Rosa held them up to show me. "I'm going to wear them to my nephew's graduation," she said. "They're not the most comfortable, but aren't they pretty?"

Analysts Reflect on Reverie

> Shame should be reserved for the things we choose to do, not the circumstances that life puts on us.
>
> —Ann Patchett, *Truth and Beauty*

When we meet Rosa, she is a young woman accustomed to hiding herself from others, including her therapist. We are struck by the discordance between Rosa's obsequious presentation and her therapist's arousal of irritation, disdain, even cruelty in her private musings. Rosa's therapist is also persistently drawn to and critical of her patient's *black, scuffed, lace-up shoes with no style,* even though she has the same shoes.

Rosa, we soon learn, was injured in a car accident when she was five, which left her with a deep scar on her cheek. Crying and separated from her mother for surgery, with no comfort offered by a cold-hearted nurse, Rosa's trauma was magnified. Any trauma can be mediated by the comforting presence of another who holds us in our pain, but this was not Rosa's hospital experience (Stolorow 2011). Rosa enters treatment for feelings of depression but soon is able to describe *the world* [as] *a mirror, reflecting back a distorted version of herself—ugly and damaged.*

When the therapist asks Rosa a question about physical pain during her convalescence, Rosa is startled, and she remembers her mother leaning over her in tears, applying ice packs. *Suddenly I see a thrashing, screaming toddler lying on her back in her crib. That toddler is me. My mother stands over me, helplessly crying. She is trying to jam my misshapen feet, curved inward like boomerangs (the effects of metatarsus adductus) into stiff leather shoes.* The therapist's memories continue to emerge: of pain from wearing orthopedic shoes her mother forced on her feet daily, of downstairs neighbors annoyed by her heavy tread.

Early in this story, the therapist recognizes that Rosa is vulnerable, but her empathy is blocked. Only when reverie brings her to her own childhood pain and the lingering impact into adolescence of feeling *trapped in ugly, uncomfortable, lace-up shoes* does something shift in her empathic stance and in Rosa's treatment. *Now, sitting with Rosa, my irritation suddenly dropped away, and in its place I felt compassion for the suffering she had endured and the scar she could not erase. An old reservoir of pain had opened up inside of me, and I saw clearly what she had been trying to tell me—and why I could not hear her.*

While initially impatient and even irritated by Rosa's shame, her therapist ultimately can speak to it more deeply and empathically once she connects with her own similar shame. As Donna Orange (2008) writes, "Shame in the analytic system belongs neither to the patient nor to the analyst, but is intersubjectively generated, maintained, exacerbated, and, we hope, mitigated within the relational system" (84). Remembering her own issues from childhood, Rosa's analyst self-reflects: *my childhood shame about my body and its deformities had resonated with her pain outside of my awareness. Instead of empathizing with her, my mind had pushed away my shameful memory and, with it, Rosa's pain.* Once she is able to hear—and bear— Rosa's pain, there is a shift in the intersubjective space.

Malcolm Slavin and Daniel Kriegman (1998) posit that the analyst must change in order for the patient to change. In their view, the patient compels us to recognize something of their painful experience in our own subjective history. As analysts, we must be willing to go to places within ourselves—to a memory stirred, to a trauma consigned to the past—and allow it to inhabit the intersubjective space in order to understand our patients' struggles. This is a pathway toward authentic empathy.

Analytic reveries offer rich potential for understanding ourselves and our patients. Rather than dismiss our various internal musings, if we pursue them, our private thoughts might bring us to places within ourselves that may have been long forgotten or set aside. There is a deep reverberation in the comingling of the subjectivities of analyst and patient. We can think of the "analytic third" as the unconscious of the patient communicating with the unconscious of the analyst.

Thomas Ogden (1994) presents his idea of the analytic third, which is the intersubjective psychological space created by the separate subjectivities of patient and the analyst:

> A major dimension of the analyst's psychological life in the consulting room with the patient takes the form of reverie concerning the ordinary, everyday details of his own life . . . reveries [that] are not simply reflections of inattentiveness, narcissistic self-involvement, unresolved emotional conflict . . . [but instead represent] the unarticulated (and often not yet felt) experience of the analysand as they are taking form in the intersubjectivity of the analytic pair (i.e., in the analytic third).

> (12)

As analysts, we come to know our patients more fully through our own internal associative and self-reflective process. Steven Cooper (2014) describes "the exchange of the patient's and analyst's reverie, a third subjectivity that is unconsciously generated by the analytic pair" (633). Judy Krantowitz (1996), in her research with close to four hundred analysts, writes about the patient's impact on the analyst. She explores "triggers for self-knowledge" that alert analysts to an experience within themselves that requires more self-examination: "As the analyst becomes increasingly clear how a particular issue that a patient is working on is also a personal one for the analyst, not yet mastered, it also gradually becomes clear how this shared aspect is, in some ways, the same for patient and analyst, and in some ways different" (52).

Rosa's therapist intuitively knew that the shoes Rosa wore reflected her feelings about herself. *I think to myself with a silent chuckle, I'll know she is ready to end analysis when she stops wearing such ugly shoes!* And then one day, Rosa, no longer timidly peering into the analyst's office, marches through the doorway to share her excitement over the elegant new shoes she has just bought.

This chapter's vignette demonstrates the interplay between the two participants in the therapeutic relationship. The analyst's willingness to use her own internal musings to bring her to a new understanding of pain and shame—both in herself and in her patient—supports Cooper's (2014) claim that "it is in this self-with-other and self-reflective space that we breathe in the psychoanalytic process" (634).

15 THE LIMO RIDE

Mary, a small, freckled, nine-year-old girl, sits across from me. Her feet barely touch the floor.

Six months after her mother died of cancer, her father called me, worried that Mary's sadness and withdrawal were deepening. He told me that Mary, an only child, had always been outgoing and a good student, but since her mother died, she had lost interest in her schoolwork and playing with friends.

Mary was similarly tentative with me. Quietly she'd sketch, periodically punctuating our sessions with thoughts of her mother and the cancer that killed her. She spoke of the unfairness—*no other* child she knew had experienced this kind of loss. Those words held a particular poignancy for me, having lost my own mother at that same age.

I was hoping that in time Mary would find our sessions a safe place to talk and share her grief so that she could find her way back to the mostly happy, secure child she had been before her mother's death. Yet rather than opening up, Mary grew more remote. To most of my comments and interpretations, she would just shrug and continue sketching.

Five months into treatment, Mary sat drawing—a new picture—a long, luxurious car.

"That's a very fancy car," I said.

She nodded. "I went in a car like this to my mother's funeral."

Immediately I was transported back to when I was nine years old, when my mother had been killed in a car accident. I recalled setting my mind to what could be the silver lining, something my mother always said I should look for in a bad situation. And I found it: I would get to ride in a limousine to the funeral. I imagined a driver, wearing a black cap and suit, bowing as he opened the door for me. There I would sit, upon fur-covered seats, like Eloise at the Plaza Hotel. But as quickly as the fantasy appeared, so had the burning shame. How terrible I was to even think about wanting to ride in a limousine when my mother was in a casket in the car ahead of me! I never told anyone about my secret wish.

As Mary continued drawing, I weighed what it would mean to reveal my experience to her. In my decades of practice, working with children and adults who had lost a parent, I had never shared that I had lost my mother when I was so young. I had never felt internal pressure to reveal this information nor sought pleasure or relief in telling my story.

I considered using my experience to inform my interpretation, maybe saying something like, "I imagine some kids might be excited to drive in a limousine but then feel bad that it was going to a funeral." But then I reflected on what it would mean *not* to tell Mary of my parallel experience—to sit silently with my own memory, so close to hers, yet say nothing. It felt inauthentic. I wondered whether, by sharing this information, I could provide her some comfort in knowing she wasn't the only one to lose a mother at such an early age—that her feelings of pleasure in getting special attention for the loss were not unexpected or shameful. That she wasn't alone? Of course, I understood that what might be the right choice in this session could cause problems, down the road, in another.

In the end, I decided to tell her: "You know, Mary, seeing the limousine reminds me of something. Something I haven't told you, but I thought it might be helpful for you to know. Like you, I lost my mother when I was nine, and I remember how *excited* I was to ride in a limousine to the funeral, but then I felt *so, so* terrible and ashamed. How could I think it was something good when my mother had died?"

Mary put down her pencil, her eyes wide with interest. "That's just what I wanted to do," she said. "I was so excited to ride in a limousine. I was so awful. My mom would think I didn't love her." For the first time Mary cried, then asked, "You really did the same thing?"

"Yep." I said.

Mary had lots more to talk about in this session and the ones after—about her secret shame and her guilt. For a year our work continued, with Mary voicing deeper feelings of loss and grief. She told me how she had been so angry at her mother for being sick, for not being well enough to attend school events or to make her an afternoon snack. She spoke of the jealousy she felt toward friends who still had their mothers and of how she no longer wanted to go to their homes and have to witness a mom's loving attention to a friend. And, more tentatively, eyes downcast, she let me know that after her mother became so sick, she sometimes wished her dead.

After giving voice to her painful feelings, Mary began to recall and tell me about her healthy mom, the one who knit her sweaters, and played hide-and-go-seek, and could "run faster than any other mom" she knew.

Gradually Mary's mood lightened. She spent fewer sessions talking about her mom and more about the fun of sleeping over at her aunt's house and her annoyance that her best friend, Melody, had slept over at another friend's house without her—all of the pleasures and concerns of a ten-year-old girl.

Ten years later, Mary called and asked if we could meet. It was wonderful to reconnect with this lovely twenty-one-year-old woman. She updated me about her life since we last met—college, relationships, her father's remarriage—and that she was starting medical school in the fall. "I'm going to be an oncologist," she told me with a smile. She spoke of our therapy and her appreciation for my help during that difficult time, when she was mourning her mother's death. She thanked me in particular for what she remembered most clearly—that I had shared my own similar loss. That moment had stayed with her in a powerful way, as it had with me. It helped her to know that someone else had experienced that deep loss and understood the secret guilt and shame she harbored.

So while I can't be certain that another intervention may have been just as effective, after meeting Mary ten years later and hearing from her what had resonated in her treatment, I'm glad that I decided to tell her my story.

Analysts Reflect on Self-Disclosure

> Each person's life is dominated by a central event, which shapes and distorts everything that comes after it and, in retrospect, everything that came before.
>
> —Suketu Mehta, *Maximum City*

In this chapter's vignette, we glimpse a treatment from the therapist's perspective. We see that the therapist is trying to understand how to reach nine-year-old Mary, who is struggling to feel her loss and integrate her grief after her mother's death and is becoming increasingly remote in her sessions. Her therapist is perplexed that *rather than opening up . . . to most of my comments and interpretations,* [Mary] *would just shrug and continue sketching.*

This stalemate shifts when Mary draws a new picture of the limousine that ferried her to her mother's funeral. Seeing Mary's sketch sparks a memory in the therapist, and with it, she senses a fresh point of entry to help Mary. *Immediately I was transported back to when I was nine years old, when my mother was killed in a car accident. I recalled setting my mind to what could be the silver lining, something my mother always said I should look for in a bad situation. And I found it: I would get to ride in a limousine to the funeral. . . . But as quickly as the fantasy appeared, so had the burning shame. How terrible I was to even think about wanting to ride in a limousine when my mother was in a casket in the car ahead of me!* This memory leads to the pivotal moment in Mary's treatment. Her therapist shifts from her usual well-trained and silent processing of her own thoughts and takes the risk of sharing her personal history with Mary.

It is this deeply authentic moment, a "now moment," in Daniel Stern's language (2004), that provides a turning point in the work. As Stern and his colleagues in the Boston Process of Change Study Group (1998) claim, "The vast majority of therapeutic change is found to occur in this domain" in moments in the "improvised, largely unpredictable, nonlinear movements toward mutual goals that characterize the processes of parent-infant and therapist-patient interactions" (300).

As therapists, we strive to understand these key exchanges, such as the one that unfolded between Mary and her therapist, and to determine whether a therapist's decision to share a private piece of her own childhood is wise. In this instance, did the disclosure of personal information open up the therapy? Did it enliven or deaden the treatment? Did it bring the dyad closer or create a distance between them? Did it promote greater clarity or deny it?

In this chapter's story, we get convincing evidence that her therapist's disclosure was constructive to Mary's treatment: *Mary put down her pencil, her eyes wide with interest. "That's just what I wanted to do," she said. "I was so excited to ride in a limousine. I was so awful. My mom would think I didn't love her." For the first time Mary cried, then asked, "You really did the same thing?"* Mary feels affirmed, and with a connection to her therapist, she shares more of the private thoughts she had shamefully kept hidden. The movement in treatment continues and accelerates now that Mary begins to feel understood and less alone. Mary talks more freely of her deep feelings of loss and anger, and then she begins to recall more of her mother before her illness. *Gradually Mary's mood lightened.* She was no longer distant, and her sessions began to contain *all the pleasures and concerns of a ten-year-old girl.*

The therapist weighed carefully the decision to tell Mary about her similar childhood experience. Most therapists recognize that what transpires in a therapy is complex and multilayered, that moments contain within them all that has come before as well as the new co-created narratives that follow. Anecdotally, we know that there is one element that always contributes to therapeutic change: that a patient feels cared about. The impact of this containment is impossible to quantify, but it is conveyed by our dedication, the quality of our listening, and how we communicate.

In the art of psychoanalysis, there are many truths but little certainty. Orange and Stolorow (1998) declare, "Practice and practical wisdom better suit work with human beings" (530). While there may be no theoretical consensus or hard-and-fast rules governing self-disclosure, we do have frameworks within which to consider the consequences. We recognize that *everything* we say and share in a treatment—even where we focus our attention—is shaped by our theories, our worldview, our assumptions, and our unconscious motivations. Sander Abend (1995) writes, "I am also convinced that my tactical decisions in such [self-disclosing] situations are influenced far more by irrational motives of my own, operating outside of awareness, and less by rapid and reliable assessments of the patient's needs at the moment, than I would prefer were the truth of the matter" (210). The therapist's subjectivity cannot be extricated from the clinical exchange.

Philip Ringstrom (2007) explores such "improvisational moments," recognizing that "how each of us organizes our clinical vision tends to be far more idiosyncratic to each analytic coupling" (60). Similarly, Lew Aron (1991) writes, "The question of the degree and nature of the analyst's deliberate self-revelation is left open to be resolved within the context of each unique psychoanalytic situation" (43).

Even as we aim to make the best clinical judgment of how to proceed based on the specific patient with whom we sit, we are never completely neutral or free from our blind spots. If we consider, however, that the interpersonal experience that arises in each treatment builds on "the therapeutic benefit that results from the freedom with which the analyst uses her own subjectivity" (Jacobs 2009), then we no longer need to constrain ourselves out of a fear of blind spots. There need not be so rigid a tension between a position of analytic authority and neutrality and the departures from the conventional analytic frame that allow for emotional and human responsiveness (Hoffman 1994; Jacobs 2009).

Theorists differ on what constitutes self-disclosure. Greenberg (1995) distinguishes "between deliberate, consciously intended self-disclosure" and the inevitable self-revelations that are the consequence of who we are in our presentation—the way we dress, speak, decorate our office—and the interpretations and techniques that we use. In clinical practice, we continually consider whether or not to share what we are *thinking*. We understand that our verbal and nonverbal responses, interpretations, and observations *are themselves* a form of self-disclosure, and we reveal a great deal about ourselves during therapeutic sessions. As analysts, what we choose to pursue or decide to let rest is intertwined with who we are and how we think. "Self-revelation is not an option; it is an inevitability" (Aron 1991, 40).

When the analyst in this chapter's vignette shares her experience of wanting to ride in a limousine as a child, we understand that she is going beyond the simple sharing of biographical information. She considers carefully whether her inclination to reveal her own mother's death in childhood is suspect, arising from her own need or desire to share her story. *I weighed what it would mean to reveal my experience to her. I had never felt internal pressure to reveal this information nor sought pleasure or relief in telling my story.*

Donna Orange and Robert Stolorow (1998) urge us to "ask who or what is 'the self' we consider disclosing" (532). They see disclosure as problematic only when psychoanalytic theory remains "trapped in overly concrete and reified conceptions of selfhood as isolated mind" (533). They posit, "If we treat emotional safety as our fundamental criterion, we must ask how particular forms of response affect the safety of the field. There is no routine, or default, procedure" (534).

Historically, and from a more conventional psychoanalytic perspective, the disclosure of personal information was understood to be neither beneficial nor necessary (Busch 1998; Chused 1997), uniformly problematic (Freud [1912] 1955; Easton 2004), narcissistic (Busch 1998), or a way to avoid a patient's anger and frustration through a boundary violation. Yet it may be that the risk of maintaining this clear demarcation is greater than the risk of thoughtful flexibility or "disciplined spontaneous engagement" (Lichtenberg, Lachmann, and Fosshage 2003). The analyst's risk taking and self-revelation "promotes" risk taking in the patient and contributes to therapeutic progress (Ringstrom 2007; Maroda 1999).

Importantly, therapists ask how we can act ethically and take responsibility for the complicated clinical choices we make. Ringstrom (2007) advocates a "relational ethic . . . a kind of 'checks and balances'" (85) of what we feel and think, and the actions we take, in the context of our treatments. Rather than taking a moral stance, which limits our analytic thinking and listening, or a routinely impulsive one in which we assume that self-disclosure will be clinically helpful, we can respond to our patients from a position of *integrity*—a stance that has at its foundation honesty and a consistency of values and aims. Our therapeutic listening requires curiosity, reflection, being vulnerable to getting it wrong, and remaining open to surprise. It is a creative process that expands and unlocks new possibilities. With this in mind, we reveal our *responsiveness* to our patients, sharing our *thinking* about the process unfolding between us in the most authentic, genuine way we can, without jargon, theory, or pretense.

Ten years later, Mary contacts the therapist to thank her for their work together. What she most remembered was that moment where the therapist had spoken of her own loss. *That moment had stayed with her in a powerful way. . . . It helped her to know that someone else had experienced that deep loss and understood the secret guilt and shame she harbored.* Contemporary relational analysts insist that "the mutual influence of these two subjective experiences is critical to a transformational process" (Jacobs 2009, 35). For Mary, the healing began then, when her therapist decided to reveal her nine-year-old humanness to her patient and Mary no longer felt alone.

PART FOUR
Transitions and Challenges

16 I CAN'T BELIEVE IT'S TRUE

"I've never seen a therapist before, but my internist recommended that I see one. Ever since he told me that I have Parkinson's disease, I have not been myself. I can't sleep. I walk around in a fog. I can't get my mind to make sense of it. I can't believe it's true. It's like I know it, but I don't."

Those were Eleanor's first words to me. I, too, found it hard to imagine that this vibrant, elegant, seventy-four-year-old woman sitting before me was seriously ill. While she could relay all the facts and describe in detail the course of events that led to her diagnosis—the endless doctor visits, the blood tests, the MRIs, the uncertainty and worry—she had no words or thoughts about what the illness meant for her and her future.

What she did talk about was a rich and rewarding life: a predominantly happy fifty-five-year-long marriage; her many years as a teacher; the pleasure she found in her adult children, a son and a daughter; her weekly bridge games; morning swims at the YMCA; and the hours she spent with her five grandchildren. Her face lit up as she told me about Ashley's winning soccer goal and Robbie's skill on the computer.

As our sessions continued, Eleanor would repeat that she couldn't believe she had Parkinson's disease, and she wondered whether perhaps it was all a terrible mistake. Yet her masklike face, her slow movements, and the slight tremor in her hands revealed the truth of the diagnosis. Over and over she'd say, "I can't believe it's true." Our meetings began to feel deadened, and I wondered whether her boggy thinking was another symptom of her illness.

One day Eleanor told me about the time she took her children to an amusement park. She listed the rides they enjoyed, off-handedly mentioning that the "boys" loved the bumper cars. The "boys" was said so casually that I almost overlooked it, and I wondered if her son had brought a friend along on the outing. But there was something about the way she moved her body, as if ducking a physical blow, which alerted me, and I asked, "boys?"

She looked startled. "Oh, I guess I haven't said . . . I never talk about it. I have . . . had . . . three children." She paused, her head cocked to the side as if looking at something off in the distance. "It's been almost forty years, and I still don't know how to talk about it, or even how to answer when I'm asked about my children." Tears filled her eyes. "I've told you about Alicia and Adam, but not about Matt—my youngest. He died . . . leukemia . . . Eleven . . . I can't believe it's true." With those last words, her face folded in on itself. The shift in her body was so remarkable that it seemed as if time had recalibrated, and now I was sitting with a thirty-five-year-old mother who had just lost her son. Witnessing her inconsolable sorrow, I felt a sickening jolt as if I had been stabbed in the chest. Tears came to my eyes.

The acknowledgment of Matt's death opened up a new space in the treatment. We came to understand how Eleanor's Parkinson's diagnosis had brought her back to those moments of horror when she first heard *those* words, "Your son has leukemia." And then, "Your son is dead."

Over the weeks and months that followed, Eleanor talked and talked not about her own illness but about Matt and his. At first hesitantly, in a whisper, about his pain and her agony at watching him suffer. She then talked more audibly about raging at the doctors who could not save him, at herself for not saving him, and about the ache that never goes away. I understood that in a strange way, she didn't want the pain to recede because it tied her to Matt. Like a secret pebble she carried in her pocket, she could turn his loss over and over, and it would always be there; he would always be there.

Slowly, after sessions filled with unabating grief, Eleanor began to remember the healthy Matt: the baby she held in her arms, the toddler who loved Cheerios. She recalled his love of motion—of riding his bike, of bumper cars, and roller coasters. The way he rubbed noses with her at bedtime. His laughter. She brought in pictures of Matt, so I too could appreciate the wonder of this boy.

Over the two years that we worked together, I watched Eleanor's physical symptoms worsen, yet she told me that she had become grateful for her illness. It had driven her to therapy, which enabled her to accept Matt's death—and her own—and bring him back to life.

Analysts Reflect on Frozen Grief

If I loved you less, I might be able to talk about it more.

—Jane Austen, *Emma*

In this story, Eleanor's narrative of losing Matthew was frozen into an aching, timeless space, a space with no past and no future and no words to express her sorrow. Absent a language for her grief, a narrative to share or ground her, Eleanor was hindered from fully mourning. On one level, this effort at self-protection blocked her pain, but sadly it resulted in her inability to remember her beloved son and to hold him close.

The magnitude of grief associated with the loss of a child presents particular challenges. This is a loss outside the ordinary developmental arc, in which a child outlives a parent. The expected is turned upside down, and reality as it had been known is jolted. We intuitively recognize that when a mother loses her child, she is losing an essential part of herself. To avoid the intensity of being slammed back to her unprocessed grief, Eleanor avoided mentioning her son altogether. To refer to her son in conversation—even to her therapist—was to experience the pain as if it were happening again in the present. In the face of trauma, our brains are wired to fight or flee or freeze. In our story, Eleanor froze.

"Frozen grief" is a term first used by Marie Langer to describe the pain and loss associated with political events in Argentina from 1976 to 1983. During this "Dirty War," Argentina's military, backed by the United States, caused the disappearance of tens of thousands of citizens (Reineman 2017). How can one mourn or accept a death when a body is not found and a family can not verify the loss? Likewise, when confronted with the death of a child whose existence is as essential as one's own, a mother can unconsciously refuse to accept the profound loss even though she was there at the moment of death (Malawista, Adelman, and Anderson 2011).

The struggle to accept the loss postpones mourning and keeps the mourner emotionally stuck—frozen—at the time of the incomprehensible death. While some, like Eleanor, may not speak of the loss, others may share fossilized memories—rigid and firmly held stories of sadness and trauma. We may notice our patients using language that is deadened, repetitive, or obfuscating. While these stories are of course *true*, they are conveyed in a flat matter, without any opening for new affect or a shifting perspective. As analysts, we listen for the smallest opening to unlock a space for mourning.

We understand that when the past is fossilized, the present and future become equally hardened. Change and growth can only occur when a patient has the flexibility to revise and reimagine the past, updating the narrative of their lives. Roy Schafer (1983) depicts psychoanalysis as the construction of "multiple histories" determined by the context of the retelling of an event, the questions that are asked, and efforts to comprehend the present through an ever-shifting historical account. He notes that we alter our histories of ourselves and others as we change:

> Each account of the past is a reconstruction that is controlled by a narrative strategy. . . . Accordingly, this reconstruction, like its narrative predecessor, is always subject to change. . . . New slants on the past will be developed and new evidence concerning the events of the past will become available.
>
> (193)

Eleanor's therapist first suspects something is amiss when Eleanor, who had previously indicated she had one son, refers to the plural "boys" when recounting a family outing. *There was something about the way she moved her body, as if ducking a physical blow, which alerted me, and I asked, "boys?"* This question prompts an observable memory in Eleanor. *The shift in her body was so remarkable that it seemed as if time had recalibrated, and now I was sitting with a thirty-five-year-old mother who had just lost her son.* Indeed, Eleanor's grief is so raw that her therapist is similarly filled with emotion.

It is interesting that the present-day diagnosis of Eleanor's Parkinson's disease would reawaken the earlier loss of her son. We come to see how the incomplete mourning of the earlier loss inhibits Eleanor from processing her illness. She tells her therapist: *"Ever since he told me that I have Parkinson's disease, I have not been myself. I can't sleep. I walk around in a fog. I can't get my mind to make sense of it. I can't believe it's true. It's like I know it, but I don't."* The critical link between these two traumas separated by decades is evident in the repetition of her phrase *I can't believe it's true.* The disbelief inherent in those words speaks to Eleanor's difficulty accepting news that changes her forever: the news of her son's illness and death as well as her diagnosis of Parkinson's disease.

The diagnosis poses a threat to Eleanor's sense of self-continuity, as did the death of her son. With his death she lost an essential thread in the fabric of her life story. With a disrupted self-narrative she is left untethered from who she knew herself to be, a mother of three children. Imagining a future without her son left her frozen, unable to move forward, or back. It is no wonder, then, that Eleanor would protect herself by limiting what she absorbed of Matt's death, sometimes to the point of denial.

Although Eleanor was in the early stage of cognitive decline, many people with Parkinson's Disease eventually face an incremental loss of memory alongside an equally horrifying loss of self. Without a thread connecting us to our past and to our memories, and without the ability to tie ourselves in the present to the future we anticipate, it's as if we no longer exist. Tulving (1985) determined that people with amnesia are unable to imagine a future. A shattered past, disconnected from the present, leaves them without the space or the capacity to summon any images for tomorrow. One woman with amnesia declared that her picture of the future was only "white space."

In our story, Eleanor initially presents a "white space" or blank in her life's narrative. Until *off-handedly mentioning that the "boys" loved the bumper cars*, Eleanor had omitted her deceased son from the personal history she recounted. Prompted by her therapist, Eleanor remarks, *"Oh, I guess I haven't said . . . I never talk about it. I have . . . had . . . three children." She paused, her head cocked to the side as if looking at something off in the distance.* The white space begins to fill. As Eleanor struggles to come to terms with her illness, the carefully constructed barrier to her son's death is broken, allowing grief to seep into her interior world. It is her incomplete mourning, her disavowal of loss, which has impaired her capacity to acknowledge and address the impact of her Parkinson's disease and to integrate it into her life.

How do we keep those we have lost alive in our minds? The brain's plasticity allows for the shifting of memory and the introduction of new information, allowing us to modify earlier affective reactions.

The back-and-forth experiences of recognition/denial and acceptance/ dissociation of traumatic loss, instantiated via incremental neural flexibility, pave the way for the eventual integration of the loss, at the same time keeping it in focus.

How do we understand the change in the flow of treatment? With her therapist's help, Eleanor brings the reality of her son's death into the present. Although she is *startled* by her therapist's question about the "boys," Eleanor is moved. *"It's been almost forty years, and I still don't know how to talk about it or even how to answer when I'm asked about my children." Tears filled her eyes.*

Indeed, she is more fully able to mourn this loss now than she was decades earlier. The affect that was unbearable then is tolerable in the presence of her therapist's curiosity and support. In treatment, Eleanor is finally able to loosen the hold on her fossilized grief, freeing herself for a future less hardened. *Over the weeks and months that followed, Eleanor talked and talked not about her own illness but about Matt and his.* Matthew needed to return to Eleanor in order for her to experience the loss of him in the present, to properly mourn him, and then to carry him within her. In other words, Eleanor needed to bring Matthew more consciously into her awareness to thaw the deep freeze.

Therapeutic healing requires an increasing level of affect tolerance and the development of integrative narratives. *Slowly, after sessions filled with unabating grief, Eleanor began to remember the healthy Matt.* In treatment—as in life—we revise our memories and retell our narratives to provide continuity with the past, acceptance of the present, and an anchored sense of self to meet the future. Although we can't change the past and bring a loved one back to life, this integrative process promotes a sense of agency, allowing for an expansion of the depth and breadth of experience in the present and in the future. As Freud wrote, "Mourning has a quite precise psychical task to perform: its function is to detach the survivor's memories and hopes from the dead" ([1913] 1955, 65) so that there is more freedom in the present and in the future.

We see Eleanor's story expand as she proceeds from a narrative without her lost son to an integrated and lively narrative of her life that included Matthew. *Over the two years that we worked together, I watched Eleanor's physical symptoms worsen, yet she told me that she had become grateful for her illness. It had driven her to therapy, which enabled her to accept Matt's death—and her own—and bring him back to life.*

I7 MUCKING THE STALL

When I was thirteen, I got a job at a stable, cleaning stalls and grooming horses in exchange for lessons and a daily ride. My teacher was a nationally recognized dressage horseman gifted at getting horses to perform intricate dance movements.

I loved this place: the slightly sour, slightly sweet smell of hay that greeted me when I slid open the heavy door and the way the horses looked up, ears twitching, swatting flies with their tails—and I loved how they clicked their teeth like old men resetting their dentures. My favorite horse was Chessy, a tall, regal sorrel with a straw-colored mane and tail, a gentle beauty who seemed to stand apart. Each time I rode Chessy and directed her with my heel, she sped up, and I soared.

I had been there for about a month when the owner of the barn, my teacher, crept up behind me, wrapped his arms around my waist, nuzzled my neck, and said, "Come here, dear, give old Monsieur Solomon a kiss." My cheeks burned as I pressed myself against the barn wall. I had been mucking out the stall, and the pitchfork hovered between us, safeguarding me from his advance. A wicked grin on his face, he lunged toward me, as if we were playing capture the flag, and I tried my best to outmaneuver him.

At the beginning, Monsieur Solomon, with his bushy white beard and whiskers, appeared harmless—a shopping-mall Santa whose lap, some years earlier, I would have confidently sat on for a holiday picture. But now, each time he saw me, he would kiss me on both cheeks, a greeting he insisted all Frenchmen did when saying hello. While embarrassed and uncomfortable with his warm breath on my skin, I complied, grateful for the opportunity to learn to ride from him. Even before this incident, Monsieur Solomon's greetings had become more insistent. When he leaned toward me, I'd duck out of the way, trying not to look as if I was avoiding him. Once or twice, I couldn't pull away fast enough to keep his mouth from sliding from my cheeks to my lips.

Now, safely out of his grasp, I dropped the pitchfork and tacked up Chessy. Although my heart was still pounding, I guided Chessy to the ring to begin my lesson. Monsieur Solomon approached, a scowl on his face. Was he angry that I hadn't played along? "I need to check if your pectoral muscles are strong enough," he said as he reached his hands under my armpits, close to my breasts, and began to squeeze. My insides squirmed, and I pulled my arms tight across my chest. "Riders need strong pectoral muscles. Do you want to be a serious rider or not?" After that day, I found reasons not to go to the stable. I would tell my parents that I had too much homework or that I wasn't feeling well.

A week or so after Monsieur Solomon had groped me, my father and I were sitting at the kitchen table, eating breakfast. He looked up from his newspaper and said, "Honey, you haven't been riding all week."

I avoided his questioning look and felt the blush creep up my neck and settle into my cheeks. "I just didn't feel like it."

Dad looked surprised. "Why not? You love riding!" he persisted.

"I've had a lot of homework," I mumbled.

"I don't understand. Being there was a dream come true, like having your own horse!"

Shrugging my shoulders, I said, "I don't know. I guess Monsieur Solomon made me uncomfortable."

"What do you mean, uncomfortable?" He put down the newspaper and looked right at me. "You never said anything. What happened there?"

"I don't know. He asks me to give him kisses. And," I paused, "He said he needs to check my pectoral muscles." His reaction was immediate: his eyes flashed anger, which I had rarely seen from my gentle dad.

"Are you mad at me?" I asked, suddenly unsure of myself.

"Oh, sweetie, no, no, you did absolutely nothing wrong." His words hovered in the air, but I couldn't let them in. After a minute, my father patted my shoulder and said, "Why don't you get to school—we'll talk more later."

That evening, I heard my father's footsteps on the stairs. He knocked softly on my bedroom door. "Hi, Bean," he said. "Can we talk?" He sat on my bed, took my two hands in his, and looked at me until I met his gaze. I could see the flecks of blue and green in his hazel eyes. "Solomon should never have behaved that way. You did the right thing to stay away," he said firmly. "I called him and told him in no uncertain terms that what he did to you was against the law. And that you were never going back there again."

My body relaxed, yet tears came to my eyes as I pictured Chessy. I would likely never see her again, never tend to her, never gallop her around the ring.

Analysts Reflect on Sexual Abuse

> This is an old story. There is nothing new in it.
>
> —Jane Hamilton, *Disobedience: A Novel*

In this chapter's vignette, we encounter an adolescent girl grappling with the disturbing advances of a once-trusted older man. While she was grooming horses in exchange for riding lessons, Monsieur Solomon was grooming her for his sexual violations by exploiting her respect for him.

This tale is one version of the many we hear in our consulting rooms and read about in the news. But there are others that are still hidden in darkness and shame. As therapists, we know that there are complex psychological impacts of such violations—whether a singular incident of physical and emotional intrusion or a traumatic repetitive sexual violation—on the development of adolescents and young adults, boys as well as girls.

Our storyteller first describes the stable as an oasis of happiness. At the barn, she enjoys a respite from the stresses of her adolescent world. As the story unfolds and Monsieur Solomon advances, we witness the erosion of the girl's sense of mastery, safety, and confidence. *I had been there about a month when the owner of the barn (my teacher) crept up behind me, wrapped his arms around my waist, nuzzled my neck, and said, "Come here, dear, give old Monsieur Solomon a kiss."* Her grasp of this demand from her revered teacher may be limited by her adolescent inexperience, but she immediately recognizes that something is wrong. *My cheeks burned.* Initially compliant when he kisses her on both cheeks, she looks for ways to avoid him. But Monsieur Solomon persists.

Where she previously saw a *shopping-mall Santa* in Monsieur Solomon, she now sees a *wicked grin*. By transgressing boundaries, Monsieur Solomon damages her idealized relationship with him and poisons her connection with the barn and the horses. She avoids returning altogether.

We see the young girl's confusion when she is accosted. She feels undone by this older man's attention, just as her body was starting to mature and she was beginning to experience the desire to be considered sexually attractive. Did she ask for this? Why does she feel embarrassed? Are these types of advances from a teacher normal? Did she do something wrong? Should she tell? When her father notices that she hadn't been to the barn all week and asks her about it, she is uncomfortable, ashamed, and vague. She mumbles and shrugs. She withdraws from her father and from the place she loved.

In Western culture, adolescence is the period of passage from childhood to adulthood. It is a stage with a multitude of developmental tasks. When development progresses without impingement, sexual feelings emerge, trust in one's perception of reality is consolidated, positive feelings about one's body and self-esteem evolve, and a sense of mastery grows. Peer relationships assist in strengthening the young person's autonomy to branch out from the primary family unit and to engage socially with the outside world (O'Brien 1987).

While there will be some rockiness during this period, as young people move back and forth to meet these developmental challenges, we usually see a flourishing of new capacities. At the start of our story, we get a clear sense of this girl's agency in knowing what she wanted (to ride) and that she had found a way to make that happen. Our protagonist conveys the thrill that accompanies her sense of mastery as she uses her body to control the horse she rides. *Each time I rode Chessy and directed her with my heel, she sped up, and I soared.* We sense the expansion of her adolescent self.

How will the course of her development be affected by Monsieur Solomon's transgressions? As clinicians, we see a range of responses to sexual exploitation. For those whose lives have been upended by incest or molestation, the future will likely bring complex challenges, mood changes, and difficulties in sustaining relationships. Sexual boundary violation can interfere with the formation of a solid identity (Feldman 1996; Price 1993), contribute to a diffusion of sense of self and difficulties with self-regulation (Watts 2014), and result in dissociative disorders (Lazar 1997).

Consolidating extensive research, Shoshana Ringel (2019) suggests that a developmental trauma like sexual abuse can impair one's ability to mourn a loss. She highlights the importance of a caregiver's attunement to a child's emotional state—particularly in circumstances of abuse—and notes that failure to confirm a child's reality can lead to dissociative defenses. A parent's "inability to tolerate the child's emotional needs and affective states contributes to the child's difficulty in feeling a sense of self-worth, expressing subjective experiences, and in regulating their distress" (4).

In this chapter, we see a father taking his daughter's report seriously. First, he notices that his daughter does not want to return to the barn, and then he listens attentively when she reluctantly explains the cause of her discomfort. For our protagonist, this is the critical moment in the story. How her father reacts will determine whether this is a manageable developmental roadblock or a shameful incident that sends her inward with confusion and isolation. Will her father discount her reality? She hesitates, waiting for his reaction: *His eyes flashed anger, which I had rarely seen from my gentle dad.* Unsure of herself, she asks, *"Are you mad at me?"* And her father tenderly and protectively reassures his daughter: *"Oh, sweetie, no, no, you did absolutely nothing wrong."*

We can intuitively grasp that for this girl there will be no secondary trauma. She is not doubted, blamed, or punished—which can happen with a disbelieving parent (O'Brien 1987). Her father assures her: *"Monsieur Solomon should never have behaved that way. You did the right thing to stay away."*

This young woman, as for any victim of sexual violation, will still pay a price. We hear stories from abused women and men who suffer the loss of a job, of money, of approval, of fitting in, of feeling special, of innocence, of opportunity, and of valued relationships. We treat those who are burdened by shame and self-doubt and who hide in silence, withdrawn from others. Here, the girl's losses are captured when she begins to integrate, with her father's help, what occurred in the barn. *Tears came to my eyes as I pictured Chessy. I would likely never see her again, never tend to her, never gallop her around the ring.*

This chapter's vignette spotlights the psychological power that a person in authority can hold over another. If a coach, boss, or teacher

pressures for compliance, many find it impossible to resist. Our culture teaches us not to question authority but to yield to it, to go along
and not rock the boat. And although the price of not going along is
high, with its many losses chronicled, the inner damage of yielding
is far costlier. The protagonist in our story did not have to suffer this
inner storm; she had a parent that sensed her turmoil and gently drew
it out of her. He then interceded on her behalf and called out the
abuser. With his action and his concern for her, his daughter felt heard
and respected and could face the loss.

18 TAKE HER BLOOD

By the time the ambulance reached the hospital, my father was no longer choking on the food that had lodged in his throat. That fact didn't seem relevant to the emergency room doctors, who persisted in their efforts to evaluate him.

My mind flashed to the day of the bicycle accident (had it really been ten years ago?) that had rendered him unable to speak, move one side of his body, or care for himself. It was the weekend I was to move into a new apartment with my boyfriend. I was twenty-one years old. I pulled into my sister's driveway, my mattress tied to the roof of the car and the back seat and trunk filled to the brim with boxes. My sister met me, wild-eyed. Something was very wrong. Piece by piece, I learned that our father had fallen off of his bicycle and that he was in the hospital. It did not register then that everyone thought he wouldn't survive. Instead of moving into my new apartment, my sister and I boarded a plane for home.

At the hospital, my father lay in the intensive care unit, hooked up to monitors and wires. His face and head were blotchy, bloody, and bizarrely swollen. There was a line through his head that was attached to an intracranial monitor whose numbers blinked red and cold. I rushed to his side, but the nurse held me back and murmured something incomprehensible. There was absolute silence. After many hushed conversations with the medical team treating him, I gradually understood that he was in a coma.

For the next several days, the three of us, my sister, my mother, and I, stood mutely by his bedside, bathed in the red glow of that unrelenting monitor, watching the numbers flash across the screen. My pulse seemed to be in rhythm with the machine, and I wondered if keeping my eyes glued to the screen would magically keep him alive.

My father, who'd just turned sixty-one, had wanted a new bicycle for his birthday. His friend helped him find his dream bike—a lightweight, twelve-speed Bianchi. My father said it was so light it felt like he was flying. This was before bike helmets were the norm, but it's likely that my fearless father would not have worn one. Having survived five years in Polish concentration camps, until his liberation from Matthausen at the age of twenty-one, he lived as though nothing bad could ever happen to him again. "Don't worry," he used to tease my mother. "There will always be bread on the table—and maybe a little butter too."

I have a photo of him on the weekend before his sixty-first birthday. It was Labor Day, and he was grilling corn and vegetables from his garden. The table overflowed with zucchini, the best tomatoes off the vine, and the purple eggplants that he nurtured tenderly. In the photo, he's standing at the barbeque, his arms up in a victory salute of sorts, shirtless, with a strong, hairy chest, beaming with the joy that we were all home together.

After the accident, my father was in a coma for more than a month. We didn't know then that he would never fully recover from the brain damage, which impaired his mobility, eradicated his speech, and rendered him completely dependent on others. To communicate, my father was given an electronic letter board, which projected each letter aloud as he pressed it. He was never a great speller to begin with, and with his alertness waxing and waning, a bad tremor, and erratic and fierce frustration (he sometimes threw the board halfway across the room), it could sometimes take him fifteen minutes or more to construct one brief sentence.

After this choking incident, and toward the end of my father's life, he spent a few months each year in a nursing home so that my mother could have some respite from caring for him. He was miserable, and so was I. I could not accept seeing him there, amid the demented and sour-smelling residents. On his letter board, he painstakingly spelled out: "T-E-L-L M-O-M-M-Y I W-A-N-T T-O G-O H-O-M-E."

When I was with my father, time slowed to a crawl. Eating was particularly challenging, as he had so much trouble swallowing and would often choke momentarily. We became accustomed to these events after a while. This time, however, the episode lasted long enough for the EMTs to be summoned. Suddenly there was activity everywhere. As the medics lifted him onto the gurney, he fixed me with his gaze. I felt again as I had years earlier, watching the intracranial monitor at his bedside: that his survival depended on me not blinking, not breaking his gaze, not looking away for even one second.

Now, as the emergency room doctors busied themselves around him, not talking to him, I suddenly saw him through their eyes: to them, he was a partially paralyzed, brain-damaged old man with whom they assumed they could make no contact. They spoke to him like a child, more loudly than necessary, under the assumption that he couldn't speak, hear, or comprehend.

The doctors had a hard time drawing his blood. My father had been subjected to so many blood draws over the years that his veins were unyielding. The doctors, determined to follow their protocol, murmured among themselves. With an occasional apology, they tried, again and again, to draw blood from his unwilling arms. Finally, my father waved them away and gestured to his letter board. I handed it to him, and the doctors stopped what they were doing and gathered round, impatient but curious. With a smirk, my father pointed at me. Then, he slowly spelled out: "T-A-K-E H-E-R B-L-O-O-D I-N-S-T-E-A-D. S-H-E H-A-S T-H-E S-A-M-E B-L-O-O-D A-S M-E."

The tension eased, and the doctors started to laugh. My father grinned back at them, as if to say, "You see? I'm still alive in here."

Analysts Reflect on Recognizing Resilience

Whatever does not destroy me makes me stronger.
—Nietzsche, *Twilight of the Idols*

In this chapter's vignette, we meet a man who endures staggering trauma both at the beginning and at the end of his adult life. Through his daughter, we learn that he *survived five years in Polish concentration camps until his liberation from Matthausen at the age of twenty-one.* Then, when the daughter is herself twenty-one, he suffers a bicycle accident that renders him incapable of movement or speech and leaves him completely dependent on others. He is once again a prisoner but once again demonstrates grace and resilience when he could have easily slipped into bitterness, resentment, and self-pity.

"The nature of resilience has been elusive," writes Paul Valent (1996) in his study of child survivors of the Holocaust. Of those identified as being resilient, he catalogs an attribution of lucky circumstances in the midst of tragedy, a deep will to live, a sustaining capacity to form attachments to others, the ability to hold internal representations of parents, hope, and even creative curiosity. He speaks to the poignancy of resilience—the ability to hold and integrate contradictory and shifting narratives in

> making something worthwhile of life in spite of its ravages. This includes love of life itself, the spirit of survival, stamina, courage against fear, the sustaining quality and power of love. They evoke awe for the capacities of the human mind even among those so young, and later capacities of repair and integration. One needs to admire the struggle to maintain what is essentially human, and the struggle to propagate this to others. Finally, one cannot help but admire the

life force, innocence, and love of children which could surmount the power, perversion, and evil of the worst persecution.

(532)

Luciana Lorens Braga and colleagues (2012) claim that "not only traumatic experiences, but also resilience patterns can be transmitted and developed by the second generation" (134). In fact, "the manner in which the traumatic message is conveyed or silenced by parents can have distinct repercussions on psychical working over in their offspring" (140). Those parental narratives that have cohesion include symbolic representations of the experience and demonstrate flexibility in affect. They establish the link between fragmented and detached narratives of loss in the present and unresolved loss and trauma from the past (Ringel 2019).

In the psychoanalyst Anna Ornstein's (2004) memoir about her early years in a concentration camp, she says, "It is the healthy psyche that is capable of keeping defenses in place (in this case, disavowal and isolation of affect) until such time when the self is strong and able to deal with the emotional pain associated with a particular memory" (674). Sophia Richman (2006) echoes the importance of modulating memory in "Remembering to Forget to Remember": being able to protect oneself from the psychological onslaught of incomprehensible threat, fear, and vulnerability is the leading edge of resilience. Valent (1998) observes, "Not remembering continued to be the key means of coping against the pain of traumas" (525) after they have ended.

But keeping memories at bay can only serve a temporary function and has to be modified for healthy development to ensue. Anne Adelman (1995), in her study of the transmission of Holocaust narratives to the next generation, observes the knotted tensions in survivors: "The narratives they constructed served both to reveal and to conceal their traumatic memories" (361). Parents' silence about their traumatic history left their children "simultaneously possessed and dispossessed of their historical legacy" (362). Only when parents can tolerate the painful affect generated in their children—the affect of their own disavowed pain—can there be a transformation of tragic memory into a meaningful and more integrated experience for both.

Like many children of Holocaust survivors, it is the daughter in this story that feels an urgency to piece together the fragments of her father's story. Ilany Kogan (2015) examines the critical psychological process of replacing "psychic holes [with] . . . psychic representations" (63). This working-through is recognized as essential in nurturing resilient offspring of Holocaust survivors.

> The construction of an unbroken narrative—one that fills the gaps in the offspring's knowledge, that makes it permissible to mention the unmentionable, that interweaves awareness of the realities and horrors of the Holocaust with the present—enables the offspring of survivors to uncover what was negated, and gradually gain some comfort from the split-off knowledge that has been accompanied by unacknowledged affects and fears.
>
> (74)

The daughter in this chapter's example recognizes her father's resilience. She tells us that her father, a man imprisoned by the Nazis in his youth, dreams of the bike he wants for his sixty-first birthday. Not just any bike, but *a lightweight, twelve-speed Bianchi. My father said it was so light, it felt like he was flying.* We can feel his soaring sense of freedom, and his daughter revels in it with him.

The father's delight in his family suggests the presence of an "open, loving, everyday communication" that contributes to the transmission of resilience in the offspring of Holocaust survivors (Braga et al. 2012, 137). Humor also contributes to resilience, and we see plenty of humor and delight in this story.

> The use of linguistic resources, such as jokes and comic tirades . . . makes the issue easier to address . . . [and] simultaneously serves to denounce the violence experienced. In these cases, humor may be

viewed as a sort of symbolic displacement, at once allowing the survivor to present and repudiate the traumatic experience without distancing himself or herself from it, creating something of a cushion to lessen the impact of traumatic experience.

(137)

The daughter in this story remembers her father's quip to her mother: *"Don't worry,"* he used to tease my mother. *"There will always be bread on the table—and maybe a little butter too."* There is a lightness here that nevertheless acknowledges that he has known times without food and certainly without richness.

At the end of the story, it is again with humor that the father asserts himself and makes himself visible to the doctors that assumed he was not present. When he types on his electronic letter board *"T-A-K-E H-E-R B-L-O-O-D I-N-S-T-E-A-D. S-H-E H-A-S T-H-E S-A-M-E B-L-O-O-D A-S M-E,"* the tension eased, and the doctors started to laugh. My father grinned back at them, as if to say, "You see? I'm still alive in here."

Throughout this story, we witness the warmth between a father and his daughter. Even following a traumatic accident that we assume would revive the despondency of earlier trauma, we sense the father's resilience. Seemingly without effort, he retains the delight and comfort in his relationship with his daughter—a relationship that we speculate filled some of his psychic holes.

19 ON THIN ICE

It is late February and freezing cold outside. The crackling fire casts its glow on the three of us—my husband and me, and our new baby. Bundled up in a sheep-patterned onesie, Lucy nurses contentedly, nestled in the crook of my arm. While she feeds, her tiny fist waves wildly in the air, then settles on her cheek. Lucy is our second daughter, born just four weeks earlier. I stare at her dimpled skin and her golden, newborn hair. Our older daughter, four-year-old Maisie, is upstairs, finally asleep after coaxing one more chapter of *Charlotte's Web* out of me.

Feeling blissful yet weary, I periodically glance up at the TV news that plays in the background. It's about the jury selection in the Rodney King case. How long has it been since the horror, the riots? Between choosing the best baby monitor, checking that Lucy is sleeping on her back rather than her belly, and making sure Maisie isn't feeling left out, I'd lost all sense of time.

"Next up," says the newscaster. "A family tragedy in Silver Spring, Maryland." I sit up straighter, jostling Lucy. This is only miles from our home. My eyes fasten to the screen. "Two sisters drowned earlier this afternoon when skating on thin ice near their home." My husband rests his hand on mine. We share the same rush of fear. The newscaster continues, "While the ice on Pine Lake may have looked thick enough, two young girls, ages nine and eleven, slipped through when they were skating across it. Rescue workers on the scene pulled the girls out of the icy water, but they were unable to revive either child."

I gasp. Lucy unlatches. A mother lost her children—two daughters. Unthinkable. Unbearable. "Relatives say the parents, both doctors at Georgetown University, are in shock. They ask for privacy during this tragic time." A cold chill runs through me. This could be me. This could be us. Do I know this couple? I can barely breathe. "The parents have lived in the Washington area since attending Howard University." A family photo, taken months earlier, appears on the screen. It shows a mother, hair cut to the shoulders, like mine, a father, and their two girls: A beautiful, Black family.

In a flash, my body relaxes—an instinctive release, as natural as my milk letting down for Lucy. I am safe. We are safe. I let out a long sigh. Instantly, and just as powerfully, I cringe at the source of my relief—these parents are Black, not like me after all. The ugliness of my thought hits me. I slump into the cushion and try to face it, to hold it, but it skitters away. I force myself to bring it back: I am this person—hiding behind my whiteness.

Lucy fusses. I press her to my breast, suddenly and painfully aware of all that I am feeding her.

Analysts Reflect on White Privilege and Othering

> I imagine one of the reasons people cling to their hates so stubbornly is because they sense, once hate is gone, they will be forced to deal with pain.
>
> —James Baldwin, *Notes of a Native Son*

To address the complex and destructive forces of racism and other-ing in our culture, we must first acknowledge our own racism. Indeed, the three white, female authors of this volume have the privilege of *choosing* when to think about race, how to think about race—even whether to think about it at all. We focus here on the impact of white privilege in the realms of both clinical and personal life.

As we read the preceding vignette, we are drawn into the gentle lull of a mother and her young infant. The scene is peaceful—until we are alerted to roiling racial issues on the news, playing in the back-ground. *The segment is about jury selection in the Rodney King case. How long had it been since the beating, the riots?* Our storyteller keeps the news in the background because she can. Her privilege as a white woman gives her the option to tune out police brutality toward a Black man. That this privilege comes at the expense of others is out-side her awareness. She pivots from this troubling news, turning instead to the contentment she has with her family. She succeeds in keeping it far away, three thousand miles away.

It is not until the mother hears the broadcaster's announcement about two little girls, sisters from a nearby community, falling through thin ice that the mother's tranquility is punctured. Now, fully engaged, the interplay of identity, otherness, and race surfaces. Initially terri-fied that something so tragic could happen to her family, the mother registers that the bereft family is not similar to hers after all: they are Black. In an instant, the grieving family is "othered." Her relief is pal-pable. *In a flash my body relaxes—an instinctive release, as natural as my milk letting down for Lucy. I am safe. We are safe.*

This mother's fundamental, urgent need, an instinctive imperative for survival and safety, is all the more poignant as she cradles her new baby. This primal fear leads her to distance herself from this Black family and to see them as other. Indeed, racial differentiation and racial prejudice allow for the denial of psychological similarity. In *Civ-ilization and Its Discontents* ([1930] 1955) Freud refers to such a defensive maneuver as "the narcissism of minor differences"—the hypersensitivity to and amplification of small differences across two otherwise very similar groups. While Freud understands the inclination to project one's aggressive impulses onto an enemy (not-me) in order to preserve a particular self-image, we can also understand the reaction of the mother in our story as self-preserving, allowing her to feel detached and thereby protected from someone else's tragedy.

Immediately, and with shame, the narrator realizes that the other family's Blackness is the source of her relief. *I slump into the cushion and try to face it, to hold it, but it skitters away. I force myself to bring it back.* Gurmeet Kanwal (2020) writes that outsiderness, like othering, "is all around us, among us, and within all of us. If we see it only in the other, it is only because we deny it in ourselves" (5). At this moment of othering, with its concomitant relief that washes over her, our young mother recognizes the toxic forces of racism comingling in her milk, unwittingly transmitted from generation to generation. As Isabel Wilkerson (2020) tells us in her book *Caste: The Origins of Our Discontents*, there are powerful intergenerational elements to white privilege.

Racism is rooted in hate, the wish for power, and fear. In her prose poetry book *Citizen: An American Lyric* (2014), Claudia Rankine speaks to the way Blackness becomes a container for what is split off from whiteness, the way the other becomes the degraded object. Ultimately, the disavowed attributions of the other are infused with the hated parts of ourselves, which are then projected and remain invisible to us. As analysts, we note that this comes at a cost, culturally and personally: when we render another inferior in order to maintain our own power or protect ourselves from feelings of vulnerability, we collude in a denial of our own prejudice and restrict the depth of our understanding of ourselves.

To counter this othering, we must work to hold the other (the not-me) in mind. When we forge no connection, offer no empathy, and fail to fully recognize the other's humanity, we continue to perpetuate the myth of the other. Rankine speaks to the risk inherent in this: "Because white men can't / police their imagination / black men are dying." The ultimate hazard of othering, Rankine tells us, is that it leads to a fantasy of Black people as different, inferior, dangerous, and unknowable. It is these racial stereotypes that endanger them both physically and psychologically.

James Baldwin locates the origins of racism more in white people's refusal to give up power than in their desire to hate other human beings. Similarly, Wilkerson (2020) observes that dominant groups do not readily yield their power, fearing that they themselves will tumble to the bottom of the caste system and become degraded. She cites centuries of repeated wounds and brutality resulting from the unrecognized caste system that exists in our country. She writes, "Caste is insidious and therefore powerful because it is not hatred, it is not necessarily personal. It is the worn grooves of comforting routines and unthinking expectations, patterns of social order that have been in place for so long that it looks like the natural order of things" (70).

Turning our focus to the impact of these psychological and cultural dynamics on our clinical work, as therapists we must challenge ourselves to recognize our own privilege and racially biased assumptions—to fight this perverse "natural order of things." Yet how can we think about race with our patients if we fail first to reflect on our whiteness? The descriptor "white" is not an ordinary signifier we use in describing ourselves, whether personally or professionally. Only in our encounters with patients of color does it become a chief descriptor, an identifier that we're compelled to think about. While both patient and therapist have subjective experiences of their own race, we might be inclined to focus entirely on the person of color's experience of race. The "other" is the one viewed as different, rendering race and racial subjectivity as something that belongs only to those with darker skin. While every skin has a color—no skin is white or black—the phrase "person of color" demonstrates the pervasive assumption that "whiteness" is normative. Our very language reflects the impact of European Caucasian dominance.

From our very first phone call or contact we develop hypotheses and harbor assumptions about who our patients are. Even before we meet them in person we imagine something about our patient's skin color, ethnicity, region of origin, level of education, and sexual identity. Upon meeting in the waiting room, both participants of the therapeutic dyad are affected—often outside of their awareness—by the other's skin color, age, dress, and gender; by the associations and past experiences evoked by these external characteristics; and by our surprise if the person in front of us does not fit our expectations.

When we recognize our biases, our erroneous assumptions, our defensive efforts to gloss over our privilege or our distorted attributions, we might, like the mother in our story, *cringe*. There may be moments in our clinical work when we face something in ourselves we do not like to see. *The ugliness of the thought hits me . . . I am this person—hiding behind my whiteness.*

Instead, we must strive to truly listen, to hear the power and resonance of our patient's particular story or to what they have gleaned about us. We must attend to our patients with the empathy of radical listening, an openness to considering what the world is like from their perspective. Hannelore Sudermann (2020) tells us that the concept of *radical listening* was introduced in the late 2000s, by Joe L. Kincheloe, "as a tool for tuning into others' voices without projecting one's own ideas and identity into the conversation." While we maintain an empathic connection with our patients, we must also acknowledge that we do not necessarily understand the lived experience of those with a racial identity different from our own. Such encounters in treatment can be emotionally fraught, tumultuous, and full of anguish. As Aisha Abassi (2014) writes of traversing difficult racial divides between patient and analyst, "We navigated the turbulent seas where prejudice, rooted in the innermost recesses of our minds, reigns supreme and threatens to temporarily obscure the search for meaning" (120).

Kimberlyn Leary (2008) writes that racial enactments are those interactions in which societal fantasies and assumptions about race are played out in the therapeutic encounter. We could also think of these moments as embodiments of the therapist's countertransference, which includes racial bias. In either case, the patient can feel humiliated, vulnerable, and exposed, as does the therapist in response.

As therapists and as patients, we bring our particular subjectivity, embedded in our cultural heritage and identities and in our conscious and unconscious adaptations to systemic racism, into the consultation room. These complex interactions play out in every therapeutic dyad. There remains much to learn about how our individual experiences, values, and biases influence therapeutic dynamics.

Henry Smith (2006) writes, "It is not so much a matter of when race and racism enter the consulting room, but whether and how we notice it" (4). And while race requires an added awareness and challenge for the therapist, if our focus is too much on ourselves—on our fear of saying the wrong thing or on repairing our guilt and shame—we cannot fully listen to our patient. Our goal as therapists is to listen, tolerate, contain, understand, and explore—even if we, like the mother in this chapter, shudder to see ourselves in a troubling new way.

20 VIRTUAL MOURNING

It's 5:52 a.m. I click on the link and enter the waiting room. Messages fly back and forth on a group chat in WhatsApp. "We are here," says one. "So are we." "When does it begin?" asks a third. I type, "I am here too," and wait.

Promptly at 6:00 a.m., I hear the now-familiar tone as the Zoom window opens, announcing "Joining the Meeting of Rabbi Shmuelson." He is in London; it is 11:00 a.m. there. I peer at my laptop and see the rabbi standing outside in a cemetery. Along the top of the screen, there are thirty or so tiny windows that I scroll through, looking at the images of family members and friends, all on standby.

The day looks cold and windy. The rabbi is wearing a black coat, dark glasses resting on the bridge of his nose, coattails whipping in the wind, his *kippah* askew. His hands, red with cold, grip a leather-bound prayer book that he holds open with one hand, ready to turn the pages with the other. A gold ring reflects off his right pinky finger. Yellow and pink sticky notes sprout from the pages like tiny tulips. Standing behind him and to his right are two gravediggers all in black—black face mask, black gloves, black pants, black fleece jackets. Beside the rabbi I see the wooden box, elevated on a bier above the freshly dug grave. Inside the coffin lies the body of my mother's sister, who has died not from the coronavirus but in the time of the coronavirus.

The cemetery is deserted, save for the dead whose graves are marked by tombstones lined up in rows stretching endlessly behind the rabbi. He looks out for a moment toward the faces of the mourners who have joined the Zoom funeral. "We are here to mourn the death of L. on behalf of her beloved family and friends," he shouts above the wind. His statement seems to imply, *If you're not here for this funeral, you're in the wrong Zoom meeting.* It brings to mind the moment before a plane takes off, when the pilot announces where the plane is headed—one last chance to deplane if that's not your destination.

I had only met my aunt once, when I was a young child. She and my mother had had a rift decades ago that persisted until my mother's death a couple of years ago. Yet I wanted to participate, to connect with my far-flung family, and to honor the death of my mother's sister.

Wrestling to be heard above the blustery weather, the rabbi recites the funeral prayers, bowing and rocking according to custom—yet it is as if the wind is the force for his *davening*. He begins to read the eulogy as the camera shakes from a strong gust.

The gravediggers step forward, straighten their masks, and lower the coffin into the grave. Then they step into the background and disappear from the screen. The rabbi had never met my aunt, yet there he stood, alone at her graveside, intoning the Hebrew prayers.

Occasionally he glances toward us, the mourners on the screen. He concentrates, as if trying to make out the tiny faces that stare back at him, watching expectantly. We are all supposed to be on mute, but some of us have forgotten, and the screen occasionally enlarges the image of a vocally tearful relative. One person seems to be having a conversation with someone in another room, but then the tiny red bar appears above his microphone icon.

The wind blows the rabbi's coat open and he grabs hold of it, tightening it around him, readjusting his *kippah* on top of his head. One of the gravediggers reenters the frame and says something to him. The rabbi turns around and grabs the shovel planted in a mound of dirt beside the grave. As he does so, the papers fly out of his book, blowing about in the wind. Momentarily he loses his balance while he tries to retrieve them. (It is hard to hold a shovel and a prayer book at the same time.) Squeezing the book under his arm, he lifts the shovel, digs deep into the mound of earth, and heaps the dirt over the coffin. With each shovelful, he calls out the names of the deceased's daughters and family members. The K'vorah—to return the body to the earth—is a mitzvah the living perform for the dead. Occasionally he stops to wipe his nose—I assume from the cold, but I have a fleeting worry: *I hope he is not sick.* From time to time, the screen enlarges the image of one of my cousins who has not put her screen on mute and has murmured a prayer.

At last the rabbi lays down the shovel. He turns toward my aunt's coffin and begins to recite the Mourners' Kaddish and the El Malei Rachamim, the memorial prayer. As he reads, he wipes his nose one last time and buries his hand—the one not holding the prayer book—deep inside his pocket. He looks like he is freezing. He looks desolate.

The service concludes. We all unmute.

"May her memory be a blessing to you," he intones.

"Amen," we all repeat into our devices.

He signs off. The screen reads, "The host has ended this meeting." Yes, Amen.

Analysts Reflect on Remote Connections

The best and most beautiful things in the world cannot be seen or even touched. They must be felt with the heart.

—Helen Keller

One year into COVID-19's presence among us, we pause and note its unprecedented disruption throughout the world. Illness is rampant, schools are closed, businesses shuttered, physical closeness rendered unsafe, fear of contagion escalated, and hundreds of thousands of lives lost. Ever resourceful, we have learned new ways to conduct our lives—from the welcoming of a new baby to the joys of a wedding to the sorrow of a funeral—without the comforting presence of being physically surrounded by those we love. We have adapted to telehealth visits with our physicians, to delivered dinners from our favorite restaurants, to enjoying theater and concerts streamed to us. We secure negative COVID-19 tests before celebrating a holiday with family, we gather with friends outside with masks on, and we conduct our psychotherapy practices virtually. The dramatic shifts we made initially have leveled into the ordinary daily experience of how we relate to others and live our lives.

In this chapter's vignette, we witness the impact of COVID-19 on the sacred ritual of burial. Our narrator provides an account of her aunt's funeral on another continent, a ceremony conducted on Zoom, enabling her to participate and honor her aunt's memory. *I peer at my laptop and see the rabbi standing outside in a cemetery. Along the top of the screen, there are thirty or so tiny windows that I scroll through, looking at the images of family members and friends, all on standby.*

The rabbi and gravediggers stand alone in the cemetery, *save for the dead whose graves are marked by tombstones lined up in rows stretching endlessly behind the rabbi.* Through our storyteller, we can practically feel the force of the day's winds—persistent as the virus that mandates this funeral be on Zoom—which whip at the rabbi as he offers the traditional prayers of mourning. The atmosphere is *desolate.*

And yet. There is a community of mourners gathered on screen, some quiet, some weeping, some conversing with another, some forgetting to turn off their microphones. We don't know if our storyteller would have flown across the ocean to attend her aunt's funeral were travel possible. The rabbi proceeds through the Jewish rituals, from time to time lifting his head to acknowledge the virtual mourners who bear witness. They are gathered together.

This chapter's story reminds us that in the face of tragedy, loss, and fear, basic elements of the human spirit remain: faith, fortitude, connections with one another, and for some, a connection to something greater than ourselves. As readers, we witness the centuries-old Jewish customs that mark the passage from life to death and a service that honors and confers dignity to the one who has died.

We are moved by the presence of family members scattered by distance and by history, determined to put a painful past to rest. Anne Adelman (2020) observes that this bleak moment in our history reveals the remarkable resilience of the human spirit and its capacity to adapt with honesty, ingenuity, and compassion.

But for our patients and others who struggle with loss, isolation, and grief, that resilience can be difficult to conjure. These struggles have been exacerbated by COVID-19, and as analysts, our collaborative explorations of them with our patients must now occur virtually. Just as it is for the mourners in our story, our therapeutic relationships must reside on Zoom, FaceTime, or other secure platforms designed to keep us safe (but separate). The familiar rituals of psychotherapy have been transformed, and with that transformation there has been loss.

In his twenty-year study of conducting treatments over the telephone, Mark Leffert (2003) draws our attention to the "literal and the psychological analytic space" (119) we rely on when we conduct treatment in our offices. He notes: "The office has been so much a part of the analytic setting that its meaning and presence for analyst and patient alike have not been previously explored" (119). Our offices afford our patients a space in which they can relinquish control, experience that which is painful, and feel emotionally held. The proximity to us creates a strong foundation on which an intense and safe emotional bond can be built and strengthened. Like weddings and funerals, therapeutic sessions have their own rituals: patients travel to meet us, leaving the physical space of work and family behind, wait in our waiting rooms until we invite them to enter our offices, and once there, settle into a special—let us say sacred—space. When the session ends, the process operates in reverse: we quietly support our patients as they reenter the world gradually, down the hall, through our waiting room, and onto the transition of a commute, which allows for the integration of meaning as they return to work or home.

In this unusual year, we observe how differently our patients respond to the changes in treatment space. For some, it is crucial that they "see" our new space on the screen so that they can feel anchored to it and to us and thereby rebuild any trust disrupted by the virus. For some, it offers a way to integrate their home life with their therapy sessions; we might "see" our patients' children pop into the room, or their beloved dog we've heard so much about, or be shown around the new apartment just purchased. Other patients revisit and mourn the loss they feel, missing our physical presence and being in our office, as we talk over the screen.

Kerry Malawista (2020) considers the impact of seeing our patients virtually. She recognizes that even though our transition to virtual work has gone smoothly most of the time, "we cannot overlook what is lost—the rich and complicated world of affect, with all of its physicality" (8). The flatness of the screen shortchanges the opportunities for the intuitive registration of what is communicated in the other's body. The two-dimensional meeting can leave us uncertain or unable to feel or touch our patient's verbal material in the ways we've previously been able to. We've lost some paths of input—often outside of our awareness—through which we simultaneously receive information, "integrating sensory and bodily cues that indicate subtle nuances of affect we are accustomed to absorbing in the physical presence of another" (8). Through the screen, we concentrate more sharply, trying to make up for all the data we no longer have access to.

Our visceral ways of knowing are compromised in our two-dimensional treatments. While our minds work hard to create the illusion that we are sitting with our patients, it is an illusion nonetheless. We imagine, but we cannot feel the way our patient's body tenses up when afraid; or emits certain smells, whether pleasant or noxious; or relaxes into the coordination of heart rhythms when two people are in a close, synchronous interaction (Feldman et al. 2011). Absent are some of the currents, the electricity, that can pass back and forth between two people without conscious awareness when we sit in a room together.

With those patients who suffer from an injury originating in preverbal unformulated experiences—from a time in childhood when gestures and the body's needs constituted the chief means of communication—not being physically in a room with us can pose significant challenges. As Paula Heimann (1950) states, "Our basic assumption is that the analyst's unconscious understands that of his patient's" (82).

As therapists, we can get distracted by worrying about our internet connection or by an unexpected text message appearing on our screen; we may disrupt the reverie with our patient or miss the bursts of inspiration or unanticipated imagery that rise to the surface if our mind wanders.

In this chapter's vignette, the rabbi works hard to focus on his job, standing alone at the graveside. He strives to bring honor, respect, community, tradition, and solace to those who gather to mourn from their separate homes. It is not the way it was supposed to be; it is an imperfect substitute. As he grabs the shovel, *papers fly out of his book, blowing about in the wind. Momentarily he loses his balance while he tries to retrieve them. (It is hard to hold a shovel and a prayer book at the same time.)* But he perseveres, dedicated to the sanctity of his actions.

So, too, is our clinical work during COVID-19 an imperfect substitute. We too can momentarily lose our balance without the familiar bearings our offices provide. Although we do not share our liminal physical space with our patients, we continue to sit together with a screen between us, steady in our listening, persistent in creating an honest exchange about what is lost and what is gained, committed to understanding our patients' experiences as fully as we can.

CONCLUSION: THE BRIDGE

Kerry L. Malawista

All sorrows can be borne if you put them in a story or tell a story about them.

—Isak Dineson

I began this book's introduction with the notion that so much of who we are and how we experience the world is an accumulation of memories and reminiscences that are filtered and updated through present experience. A story can never be separated from who we are in the moment of remembering, highlighting the truth that what we *feel* at the time of recollecting can literally change the memory. So, while the stories shared on these pages transpired over thirty or more years, our *remembering* them, our writing them down, occurred in 2020, a year of turmoil.

As the invisible COVID-19 virus devastated our nation and the world, we faced the impact of systemic and foundational racism in our country, the deep division between rich and poor, and the polarizing political tensions that threaten our democracy and reveal its fragility. All of these events influenced the creation of this book and the choice of stories we were compelled to share. While we set out to duplicate the tone of the original "Tutu book"—the whimsical and light-hearted stories of our past—our memories were filtered through the residues of this painful year.

Julian Barnes writes in *The Sense of an Ending*, "What you end up remembering isn't always the same as what you have witnessed." This is true for all memory, not only those of long ago. I observed the power of this truth when my friend Abe visited us. One afternoon we decided to see an exhibit at the Corcoran Museum in Washington, DC. As I climbed into the front passenger seat of Abe's car, I noticed a group of county workers repairing the sewer line—a project that required digging a massive hole in the street—in line with my driveway.

While I thought that it was stating the obvious but appreciating my friend's well-known distractibility, I said, "When you back up, don't forget to watch out for that hole." Abe started the car, then briefly paused to answer a call on his cell phone. When he resumed backing out, he drove straight into the hole. After shaking off the initial shock and seeing that we were both okay, we laughed and carefully climbed out of the car. To the side stood the crew of five, shovels in hand, staring, mouths agape, at Abe's half-visible Honda.

The men quickly went to work to figure out a way to lift the car out of the hole. As Abe and I watched, I heard one of the men say, "I can't believe that lady did that." A second barked back, "Yeah, doesn't she look where she's going?"

They were not joking. Their memory of this event, one that had occurred just minutes earlier, had already been altered. These men, like all of us, perceive things as we imagine them to be, based on our own histories and beliefs—in this instance, that only a woman could drive a car into a hole.

Memories do change. That is why two people experiencing the very same event will describe it in different ways. And when a memory doesn't fit well into the narrative we have created, we are either less likely to remember it, or we find a way to change the story. I treated a patient who returned to therapy years after our work ended when she was going through a divorce. The husband she had described in the earlier treatment as part of the *we* who had shared a hilarious visit to Graceland, or who had been thrilled at their home remodeling job, is now the singular *he* who could only take off three days for a vacation, the *he* who insisted on the cheaper cabinets whose doors now don't work. The warm memories seem to have vanished, repainted by the patient in a different shade. I felt like I was hearing about a completely different husband—the kind, loving one had been air-brushed out of the picture.

This year is a reminder that we can't change the facts of the cumulative events affecting us personally, nationally, and globally; we cannot undo the pain and sorrow millions have experienced or the many deaths we have witnessed. We can't form a narrative that leads us into the future when the underlying issues—disease, racism, xenophobia, and suffering—still thrive.

While we can't reverse the suffering endured this year, we aim to remember without denying pain or being restrained by *living* in a painful mindset of grief. Our memories shift to help us make sense of what has happened. At the same time that memories are about the past and who we are in the present, they serve as a narrative bridge carrying us forward—a bridge that provides hope when hope can barely be glimpsed. To thrive, we need a narrative that is flexible and resilient enough to be created during a year visited by a pandemic, racial strife, economic insecurity, and polarized politics and then recreated when necessary throughout our lives.

We acknowledge that the wounds of this past year are still fresh, but we don't want to stop there. Instead, I finish with a story from the spring of 2020, when the pandemic shutdown was just starting. It is a story I choose to carry with me into the future to create hope and healing.

While physically distancing from others, my husband and I took leisurely strolls through our neighborhood. Although the pandemic made our world smaller and our lives more constrained, these walks offered a few unexpected gifts: the lawn art we'd never noticed before, cherry trees in bloom, and two tree trunks carved to look like pencils. We spotted children, freed from their hectic schedules, playing hopscotch, riding bikes, and drawing on the street with chalk, no watchful parents in sight. On one of our walks, I noticed a brother and sister who looked bored on our way out, but on our return, I could see that they were busily building a fort out of sticks.

One afternoon, as we approached the local footbridge, I noticed a red and blue pompom lying on the ground; it had likely fallen off a child's winter hat. In the past I would have walked by it, but in this new pandemic mindset, the ball of spiky yarn struck me as being the very image of the COVID-19 virus. I picked up the pompom and tied it to the bridge's railing, wondering if anyone else would see this woolly virus replica the same way I did.

The next day, we took our walk, and I saw that someone had tied a ball of fabric, another virus pompom, next to mine on the bridge. I was elated! A stranger had recognized my communication and responded in kind. In the midst of fear and uncertainty, we had both found a way to delight in our shared experience. Each day, for months, I'd visit the bridge and discover more and more "viruses" tied there, a colorful festoon of others' offerings and a communication about the display I had started.

We live in a period of uncertain and rapidly shifting coronavirus tides—we have a vaccine, but we can't distribute it quickly enough; the vaccine provides some protection, but how much and for how long are unknown; while we have more knowledge about medical treatments, people are still dying at significant rates. Yet I find I am buoyed by this kaleidoscope of viral shapes that I see multiply on the bridge where I walk, like a growing chorus of human voices, singing out to one another to make contact.

It gives me hope for the future.

ACKNOWLEDGMENTS

We thank our editor, Stephen Wesley, for his thoughtful and patient guidance through the writing and publication process and Robert Fellman for his meticulous copyediting of the final manuscript. We are appreciative of the staff at Columbia University Press for their many helpful contributions and support of this book. We are grateful to Susan Graham for her meticulous, sensitive, and insightful editing of early drafts.

Most importantly, this book would not be possible without the many lessons that our patients continue to teach us. Your stories inspire us, touch us, and deepen our understanding of human vulnerability, resilience, and the capacity for change.

For that, we thank you.

We are grateful to our husbands, Alan, Norman, and Eric, for encouraging and supporting us.

NOTES

Introduction

1. When we refer to "psychotherapy," we are referencing all of the psychodynamic-oriented psychotherapies. We limit the terms *analyst* and *analysis* to those occasions when we are specifically referencing that particular treatment modality.

4. What Are You Thinking?

1. Susan Isaacs (1948) first highlighted the distinction between phantasy with a "ph," which refers to unconscious thoughts and images, as opposed to a fantasy with an "f," which refers to conscious images such as daydreams.

7. Butterfly Bandage

This story is abridged from Malawista (forthcoming).

8. Saving Swifty

This case was previously discussed in Malawista (2004).

13. Stepping Over the Threshold

1. For more on the holding environment, see Malawista, Adelman, and Anderson (2011, 113–23).

16. I Can't Believe It's True

A version of this chapter was published as Malawista (2016).

19. On Thin Ice

Some of the ideas expressed here appear in Malawista (2019).

20. Virtual Mourning

A previous version of this story was published as Adelman (2020).

REFERENCES

Abassi, A. 2014. "Sadistic Transferences in the Context of Ethnic Difference: Before and After 9/11." In *The Rupture of Serenity: External Intrusions and Psychoanalytic Technique*, 111–37. London: Karnac.

Abend, S. 1986. "Countertransference, Empathy, and the Analytic Ideal." *Psychoanalytic Quarterly* 55:563–75.

——. 1995. "Discussion of Jay Greenberg's Paper on Self-Disclosure." *Contemporary Psychoanalysis* 31:207–11.

Adelman, A. 1995. "Traumatic Memory and the Intergenerational Transmission of Holocaust Narratives." *Psychoanalytic Study of the Child* 50:343–67.

——. 2020. "Virtual Mourning." *Journal of the American Psychoanalytic Association* 68 (3): 483–86.

Adelson, M. J. 2000. "Dealing with Aging Parents." *Journal of Clinical Psychoanalysis* 9 (1): 127–36.

Agger, E. 1988. "Psychoanalytic Perspectives on Sibling Relationships." *Psychoanalytic Inquiry* 8 (1): 3–30.

Allik, T. 2003. "Psychoanalysis and the Uncanny: Take Two or When Disillusionment Turns Out to Be an Illusion." *Psychoanalysis and Contemporary Thought* 26 (1): 3–37.

Akhtar, S. 2013. *Psychoanalytic Listening*. London: Karnac.

Altschul, S. 1988. *Childhood Bereavement and Its Aftermath*. Madison, CT: International Universities Press.

American Psychological Association Zero Tolerance Task Force. 2008. "Are Zero Tolerance Policies Effective in the Schools?" *American Psychologist*, December 2008, 852–62.

Arnold, K. 2012. "Humming Along: The Meaning of Mm-Hmm in Psychotherapeutic Communication." *Contemporary Psychoanalysis* 48 (1): 100–17.

Aron, L. 1991. "The Patient's Experience of the Analyst's Subjectivity." *Psychoanalytic Dialogues* 1:29–51.

——. 2000. "Self-Reflexivity and the Therapeutic Action of Psychoanalysis." *Psychoanalytic Psychology* 1 (4): 667–89.

Bacal, H. 1998. "Optimal Responsiveness and the Therapeutic Process." In *Optimal Responsiveness: How Therapists Heal their Patients*, ed. H. Bacal, 249–70. Hillsdale, NJ: Jason Aronson.

Bacal, H., and B. Herzog. 2003. "Specificity Theory and Optimal Responsiveness: An Outline." *Psychoanalytic Psychology* 20:635–48.

Bach, S. 2001. "On Being Forgotten and Forgetting One's Self." *Psychoanalytic Quarterly* 70 (4): 739–56.

Baldwin, J. 1955. *Words of a Native Son*. Boston: Beacon.

Balint, A. 1943. "Identification." *International Journal of Psychoanalysis* 24:97–107.

Balint, M. 1968. *The Basic Fault*. New York: Brunner/Mazel, 1979.

Balsam, R. 2013. "Sibling Interaction." *Psychoanalytic Study of the Child* 67:635–52.

Beebe, B., and F. M. Lachmann. 2002. *Infant Research and Adult Treatment: Co-constructing Interactions*. Hillsdale, NJ: Analytic Press.

——. 2013. *The Origins of Attachment*. New York: Routledge.

Bettelheim, B. 1976. *The Uses of Enchantment*. London: Peregrine.

Bion, W. R. 1959. "Attacks on Linking." *International Journal of Psychoanalysis* 40:308–15.

——. 1962. "The Psychoanalytic Study of Thinking." *International Journal of Psychoanalysis* 43:306–10.

——. 1963. *Elements of Psychoanalysis*. New York: Basic Books.

——. 1967. "Notes on Memory and Desire." *Psychoanalytic Forum* 2:271–80.

Blos, P. 1962. *On Adolescence: A Psychoanalytic Interpretation*. New York: Free Press of Glencoe.

——. 1967. "The Second-Individuation Process of Adolescence." *Psychoanalytic Study of the Child* 22:162–86.

——. 1976. "The Split Parental Imago in Adolescent Social Relations—An Inquiry Into Group Psychology." *Psychoanalytic Study of the Child* 31:7–33.

——. 1987. "The Second Individuation Process of Adolescence." *Psychoanalytic Study of the Child* 22:162–86.

Bollas, C. 1987. *The Shadow of the Object: Psychoanalysis of the Unthought Known*. London: Free Association.

——. 1992. *Being a Character: Psychoanalysis and Self-Experience*. New York: Hill and Wang.

Bolognini, S. 2009. "The Complex Nature of Psychoanalytic Empathy: A Theoretical and Clinical Exploration." *Fort Da* 15:35–56.

Bowlby, J. 1960. "Grief and Mourning in Infancy and Early Childhood." *Psychoanalytic Study of the Child* 15:9–52.

Braga, L. L., F. M. Mello, and J. P. Fiks. 2012. "Transgenerational Transmission of Trauma and Resilience: A Qualitative Study with Brazilian Offspring of Holocaust Survivors." *BMC Psychiatry* 12:134–42.

Bromberg, P. 1998. *Standing in the Spaces*. Hillsdale, NJ: Analytic Press.

Buechler, S. 2012. *Still Practicing*. New York: Routledge, 2012.

Busch, F. 1998. "Self-Disclosure Ain't What It's Cracked Up to Be." *Psychoanalytic Inquiry* 18 (4): 518–29.

Casement, P. 2006. *Learning from Life*. Sussex: Routledge.

Chused, J. F. 1997. "The Patient's Perception of the Analyst's Self-Disclosure: Commentary on Amy Lichtblau Morrison's Paper." *Psychoanalytic Dialogues* 7 (2): 2243–56.

Claparède, E. 1911. *Experimental Pedagogy and the Psychology of the Child*. Bristol: Thoemmes.

Coates, S. 1998. "Having a Mind of One's Own and Holding the Other in Mind: Commentary on Paper by Peter Fonagy and Mary Target." *Psychoanalytic Dialogues* 8 (1): 115–48.

Cooper, S. H. 2014. "The Things We Carry: Finding/Creating the Object and the Analyst's Self-Reflective Participation." *Psychoanalytic Dialogues* 24 (6): 621–36.

Cournos, F. 2001. "Mourning and Adaptation Following the Death of a Parent in Childhood." *Journal of American Academy of Psychoanalysis* 29:137–45.

Dalal, F. 2008. "Against the Celebration of Diversity." *British Journal of Psychotherapy* 24 (1): 4–19.

Damasio, A. 2000. *The Feeling of What Happens: Body and Emotion in the Making of Consciousness*. New York: Houghton Mifflin Harcourt.

Davies, R. 2018. "Rivalry: Benign or Belligerent Sibling of Envy and Jealousy? A Clinical Reflection on the 'Winded, Not Wounded' Experience in the Countertransference." *Psychoanalytic Quarterly* 87 (2): 265–86.

De Peyer, J. 2016. "Uncanny Communication and the Porous Mind." *Psychoanalytic Dialogues* 26 (2): 156–74.

Diangelo, R. 2018 *White Fragility*. Boston: Beacon.

Easton, J. 2004. "Life Changes, Analytic Changes Revisited: Current Perspectives on Their Relationship." *Journal of the American Psychoanalytic Association* 52 (4): 1025–40.

Einstein, A. 1935. *The World as I See It*. London: Bodley Head.

Fairbairn, W. R. D. 1940. "Schizoid Factors in the Personality." In *An Object-Relations Theory of the Personality*, 3–27. London: Routledge, 1954.

——. 1941. "A Revised Psychopathology of the Psychoses and Psychoneuroses. In *An Object-Relations Theory of the Personality*, 28–58. London: Routledge, 1954.

Feldman, B. 1996. "Identity, Sexuality, and the Self in Late Adolescence." *Journal of Analytical Psychology* 41 (4): 491–507.

Feldman, R., R. Magori-Cohen, G. Galili, M. Singer, and Y. Louzoun. 2011. "Mother and Infant Coordinate Heart Rhythms Through Episodes of Interaction Synchrony." *Infant Behavioral Development* 34:569–77.

Ferenczi, S. 1909. "Introjection and Transference." In *First Contributions to the Theory and Technique of Psychoanalysis*, trans. Ernest Jones, 30–79. London: Karnac, 1952.

——. 1928. "The Elasticity of Psychoanalytic Technique." In *Selected Papers*, ed. J. Borossa, 3:255–68. New York: Penguin, 1999.

——. 1933. "Confusion of Tongues Between Adults and the Child. The Language of Tenderness and of Passion." In *Final Contributions to the Problems and Methods of Psycho-analysis*, 156–67). London: Karnac, 1980.

Fliess, R. 1942. "The Metapsychology of the Analyst." *Psychoanalytic Quarterly* 11:221–27.

Fonagy, P. 1989. "On Tolerating Mental States: Theory of Mind in Borderline States." *Bulletin of the Anna Freud Centre* 12 (2): 91–115.

——. 1991. "Thinking About Thinking: Some Clinical and Theoretical Considerations in the Treatment of a Borderline Patient." *International Journal of Psychoanalysis* 72:639–56.

Fonagy, P., and M. Target. 1996. "Playing with Reality: I. Theory of Mind and the Normal Development of Psychic Reality." *International Journal of Psychoanalysis* 77:217–33.

——. 1998. "Mentalization and the Changing Aims of Child Psychoanalysis." *Psychoanalytic Dialogues* 8:87–114.

Foreman, S. 2018. "Pathological Identification." *Psychoanalytic Psychology* 35 (1): 15–30.

Formanek, R. 1986. "Learning the Lines: Women's Aging and Self Esteem." In *Psychoanalysis and Women: Contemporary Reappraisals*, ed. J. Alpert, 139–60. Hillsdale, NJ: Analytic Press.

Fosshage, J. 1995. "Countertransference as the Analyst's Experience of the Analysand: Influence of Listening Perspectives." *Psychoanalytic Psychology* 12:375–91.

Frankel, J. 2002. "Exploring Ferenczi's Concept of Identification with the Aggressor: Its Role in Trauma, Everyday Life, and the Therapeutic Relationship." *Psychoanalytic Dialogues* 12 (1): 101–39.

Frankiel, R. V., ed. 1994. *Essential Papers on Object Loss*. New York: New York University Press.

Freud, A. 1937. *The Ego and the Mechanisms of Defence*. London: Karnac.

Freud, S. [1900] 1953. *The Interpretation of Dreams*. SE 4:1–626. London: Hogarth.

——. [1905] 1955. "Jokes and Their Relation to the Unconscious." *SE* 8:1–247. London: Hogarth.

——. [1912] 1955. "Recommendations to Physicians Practicing Psychoanalysis." *SE* 12:1–124. London: Hogarth.

——. [1913] 1955. *Totem and Taboo*. *SE* 13:1–161. London: Hogarth.

——. [1913] 1963. "Further Recommendations in the Technique of Psychoanalysis: On Beginning the Treatment." In *Freud: Therapy and Technique*, ed. P. Rieff. New York: Macmillan.

——. [1917] 1955. "Mourning and Melancholia." *SE* 14:237–58. London: Hogarth.

——. [1919] 1955. "The Uncanny." *SE* 17:217–56. London: Hogarth.

——. [1922] 1955. *Group Psychology and the Analysis of the Ego*. SE 18:69–144. London: Hogarth.

——. [1926] 1959. *Inhibitions, Symptoms, and Anxiety*. SE 20:77–175. London: Hogarth.

——. [1930] 1955. *Civilization and Its Discontents*. SE 21:57–146. London: Hogarth.

——. [1933] 1955. "Dreams and Occultism." *SE* 22:31–56. London: Hogarth.

Fuchs, T. 2011. "Body Memory and the Unconscious." In *Founding Psychoanalysis Phenomenologically*, ed. D. Lohmer and J. Brudzińska, 69–82. London: Springer.

Furman, E. 1981. *A Child's Parent Dies: Studies in Childhood Bereavement*. New Haven, CT: Yale University Press.

———. 1986. "On Trauma—When Is the Death of a Parent Traumatic?" *Psychoanalytic Study of the Child* 41:191–208.

Furman, R. A. 1964. "Death and the Young Child—Some Preliminary Considerations." *Psychoanalytic Study of the Child* 19:321–33.

Furman, R. A. [1968] 1994. "Additional Remarks on Mourning and the Young Child." In *Essential Papers on Object Loss*, ed. R. V. Frankiel, 363–75. New York: New York: University Press.

Gabbard, G. O. 1982. "The Exit Line: Heightened Transference-Countertransference Manifestations at the End of the Hour." *Journal of the American Psychoanalytic Association* 30:579–98.

Gallese, V. 2001. "The 'Shared Manifold' Hypothesis: From Mirror Neurons to Empathy." *Journal of Consciousness Studies* 8 (5–7): 33–50.

Garber, B. 2008. "Mourning in Children: A Theoretical Synthesis and Clinical Application." *Annual of Psychoanalysis* 36:174–88.

Gediman, H. 2006. "Facilitating Analysis with Implicit and Explicit Self-Disclosures." *Psychoanalytic Dialogues* 16 (3): 241–62.

Geist, Richard. 2007. "Who Are You, Who Am I, and Where Are We Going: Sustained Empathic Immersion in the Opening Phase of Psychoanalytic Treatment." *International Journal of Psychoanalytic Self Psychology* 2:1–26.

Geller, J. D. 2003. "Self-Disclosure in Psychoanalytic-Existential Therapy." *Journal of Clinical Psychology* 59 (5): 541–54.

Gerson, M. J. 2018. "Death of a Parent: Openings at an Ending." *Psychoanalytic Perspectives* 15 (3): 340–54.

Greenberg, J. 1995. "Self-Disclosure: Is It Psychoanalytic?" *Contemporary Psychoanalysis* 31 (2): 193–205.

Greenson, R. 1960. "Empathy and Its Vicissitudes." *International Journal of Psychoanalysis* 41:418–24.

Grossmark, R. 2012. "The Unobtrusive Relational Analyst." *Psychoanalytic Dialogues* 22 (6): 629–46.

Hall, J. 1988. *Deepening the Treatment*. Northdale, NJ: Jason Aronson.

Hamilton, J. 2001. *Disobedience*. New York: First Anchor.

Heimann, P. 1950. "On Counter-transference." *International Journal of Psychoanalysis* 31:81–84.

Hoffman, I. Z. 1994. "Dialectical Thinking and Therapeutic Action in the Psychoanalytic Process." *Psychoanalytic Quarterly* 63:187–218.

——. 1998. *Ritual and Spontaneity in the Psychoanalytic Process.* New York: Analytic Press.

Howe, J. 1990. *There's a Monster Under the Bed.* New York: Atheneum Books for Young Readers.

Howell, E. 2005. *The Dissociative Mind.* New York: Routledge.

Isaacs, S. 1948. "The Nature and Function of Phantasy." *International Journal of Psychoanalysis* 29:73–97.

Jacobs, L. 2009. "Meeting Beyond the Frame: Extraordinary Demands and Analytic Choices." *Psychoanalytic Perspectives* 6:32–44.

Jacobs, T. J. 1991. *The Use of the Self: Countertransference and Communication in the Analytic Situation.* Madison, CT: International Universities Press.

——. 1993. "The Inner Experiences of the Analyst: Their Contribution to the Analytic Process." *International Journal of Psychoanalysis* 74:7–14.

——. 2007. "Listening, Dreaming, Sharing: On the Uses of the Analyst's Inner Experiences." In *Listening to Others: Developmental and Clinical Aspects of Empathy and Attunement,* ed. S. Akhtar, 93–112. Lanham, MD: Jason Aronson.

——. 2012. "Travels with Charlie: On My Long-Standing Affair with Theory." *Psychoanalytic Inquiry* 32:60–68.

Jentsch, E. 1906. "On the Psychology of the Uncanny." Trans. Roy Sellars. http://www.art3idea.psu.edu/locus/Jentsch_uncanny.pdf.

Kanefield, L. 1985. "Feminist Values and Psychoanalysis: The Patient's Curative Capacities." In *Yearbook of Psychoanalysis and Psychotherapy,* ed. R. Langs, 1:3–24.

Kantrowitz, J. 1996. *The Patient's Impact on the Analyst.* Northdale, NJ: Analytic Press.

——. 2009. "Privacy and Disclosure in Psychoanalysis." *Journal of the American Psychoanalytic Association* 57 (4): 787–806.

Kanwal, G. S. 2020. "Outsiderness: A Meditation in Six Visions." *Contemporary Psychoanalysis* 56 (2): 1–13.

Katz, P. A., and J. A. Kofkin. 1997. "Race, Gender, and Young Children." In *Developmental Psychopathology on Adjustment, Risk, and Disorder*, ed. S. S. Luthar and J. A. Burack, 51–74. New York: Cambridge University Press.

Keats, J. 2002. "Letter to George and Thomas Keats, December 22, 1817." In *Selected Letters*, 41–42. New York: Oxford University Press.

Kernberg, O. 1994. "Validation in the Clinical Process." *International Journal of Psychoanalysis* 75:1193–1200.

Klein, M. [1937] 1975. "Love, Guilt, and Reparation." In *Love, Guilt, and Reparation and Other Works*. New York: Delta.

——. 1940. "Mourning and Its Relation to Manic-Depressive States." *International Journal of Psychoanalysis* 21:125–53.

——. 1946. "Notes on Some Schizoid Mechanisms." *International Journal of Psychoanalysis* 27:99–110.

Koff, R. H. 1961. "A Definition of Identification: A Review of the Literature." *International Journal of Psychoanalysis* 42:362–70.

Kogan, I. 2015. "From Psychic Holes to Psychic Representations." *International Forum of Psychoanalysis* 24 (2): 63–76.

Kohut, H. [1959] 1978. "Introspection, Empathy, and Psychoanalysis: An Examination of the Relationship Between Mode of Observation and Theory." In *The Search for the Self: Selected Writings of Heinz Kohut: 1950–1978*, ed. P. Ornstein. New York: International Universities Press.

——. 1977. *The Restoration of the Self*. New York: International Universities Press.

Kohut, H., A. Goldberg, and P. Stephansky. 1984. *How Does Analysis Cure?* Chicago: University of Chicago Press.

Lamont, J. 2013. "Out-of-School Suspension and Expulsion." *Pediatrics* 131 (3): 1000–7.

Langer, M. 1981. "Between the Imaginary and the Real: Photographic Portraits of Mourning and of Melancholia in Argentina." *International Journal of Psychoanalysis* 92 (5): 1241–61.

Lazar, S. 1997. "Epidemiology of Mental Illness in the United States: An Overview of the Cost Effectiveness of Psychotherapy for Certain Patient Populations." *Psychoanalytic Inquiry* 17S: 4–16.

Leary, K. 2000. "Racial Enactments in Dynamic Treatment." *Psychoanalytic Dialogues* 10 (4): 639–53.

LeCoq, J. 1997. *The Moving Body: Teaching Creative Theatre*. New York: Routledge.

Leffert, M. 2003. "Analysis and Psychotherapy by Telephone: Twenty Years of Clinical Experience." *Journal of the American Psychoanalytic Association* 51 (1): 101–30.

Leichtman, M. 1985. "The Influence of an Older Sibling on the Separation-Individuation Process." *Psychoanalytic Study of the Child* 40:111–61.

Levine, S. S. 2007. "Nothing but the Truth: Self-Disclosure, Self-Revelation, and the Persona of the Analyst." *Journal of the American Psychoanalytic Association* 55 (1): 81–104.

Lichtenberg, J. 1981. "The Empathic Mode of Perception and Alternative Vantage Points for Psychoanalytic Work." *Psychoanalytic Inquiry* 1:329–56.

——. 1992. "Interpretive Sequence." *Psychoanalytic Inquiry* 12 (2): 248–74.

Little, M. 1951. "Counter-transference and the Patient's Response to It." *International Journal of Psycho-Analysis* 32:32–40.

Malawista, K. 2004. "Rescue Fantasies in Child Therapy." *Child and Adolescent Social Work Journal* 21 (4): 373–86.

——. 2016. "Finding the Words." *Intima: Journal of Narrative Medicine*. Fall.

——. 2019. "Imagining the Other." *ROOM: A Sketchbook for Analytic Action* 2:19, https://www.analytic-room.com/essays/imagining-the-other-kerry-malawista/.

——. 2020. "Are You Still There?" *TAP: The American Psychoanalyst* 54 (30): 7–8.

——. Forthcoming. *Meet the Moon*. Regal House.

Malawista, K., A. J. Adelman, and C. Anderson. 2011. *Wearing My Tutu to Analysis and Other Stories: Learning Psychodynamic Concepts from Life*. New York: Columbia University Press.

Maroda, K. J. 1999. "Creating an Intersubjective Context for Self-Disclosure." *Smith College Studies in Social Work* 69 (2): 474–89.

Mayer, E. L. [1958] 1996. "Changes in Science and Changing Ideas About Knowledge and Authority in Psychoanalysis: Werner Heisenberg." *Psychoanalytic Quarterly* 65:158–200.

——. 1996a. "Subjectivity and Intersubjectivity." *International Journal of Psychoanalysis* 77:709–37.

——. 2001. "On 'Telepathic Dreams?': An Unpublished Paper by Robert J. Stoller." *Journal of the American Psychoanalytic Association* 49 (2): 629–57.

——. 2007. *Extraordinary Knowing: Science, Skepticism, and the Inexplicable Powers of the Human Mind.* New York: Bantam.

McMorris, B., K. Beckman, G. Shea, J. Baumgartner, and R. Eggert. 2013. "Applying Restorative Practices to Minneapolis Public Schools Students Recommended for Possible Expulsion." In *Final Report December 2013.* Healthy Youth Development, Prevention Research Center.

Meissner, W. W. 2000. "On Analytic Listening." *Psychoanalytic Quarterly* 69:317–67.

——. 2002. "The Problem of Self-Disclosure in Psychoanalysis." *Journal of the American Psychoanalytic Association* 50 (3): 827–67.

Mendelsohn, E. 2018. "First Meetings in Therapy: Poetics and Pragmatics." Paper presented at ICP+P Annual Conference. https://icpeast.org/may5/.

Mitchell, J. 2003. *Siblings: Sex and Violence.* Cambridge: Polity.

Mitchell, S. 2000. *Relationality: From Attachment to Intersubjectivity.* Northvale, NJ: Analytic Press.

Morrison, A. 1984. "Working with Shame in Psychoanalytic Treatment." *Journal of the American Psychoanalytic Association* 32:479–505.

——. 1994. "The Breadth and Boundaries of a Self-Psychological Immersion in Shame: A One-and-a-Half-Person Perspective." *Psychoanalytic Dialogues* 4 (1): 19–35.

——. 1999. "Shame, on Either Side of Defense." *Contemporary Psychoanalysis* 35 (1): 91–105.

Moore, B., and B. Fine. 1990. *Psychoanalytic Terms and Concepts*. New York: American Psychoanalytic Association.

Newberger, J. 2015. "The (K)not of Self-Disclosure: One Therapist's Experience." *Psychoanalytic Social Work* 22 (1): 39–51.

Novick, K. K., and J. Novick. 2013. "Concurrent Work with Parents of Adolescent Patients." *Psychoanalytic Study of the Child* 67:103–36.

O'Brien, J. O. 1987. "The Effects of Incest on Female Adolescent Development." *Journal of the American Academy of Psychoanalysis* 15 (1): 83–92.

Ogden, T. H. 1979. "On Projective Identification." *International Journal of Psychoanalysis* 60:357–73.

——. 1994. "The Analytic Third: Working with Intersubjective Clinical Facts." *International Journal of Psychoanalysis* 75:3–19.

——. 1997. "Reverie and Interpretation." *Psychoanalytic Quarterly* 66:567–95.

Orange, D. 2008. "Whose Shame Is It Anyway: Lifeworlds of Humiliation and Systems of Restoration (Or 'The Analyst's Shame')." *Contemporary Psychoanalysis* 44 (1): 83–100.

Orange, D., and R. Stolorow. 1998. "Self-Disclosure from the Perspective of Intersubjectivity Theory." *Psychoanalytic Inquiry* 18:530–37.

Ornstein, A. 2004. *My Mother's Eyes*. Cincinnati, OH: Emmis.

Ornstein, P., and A. Ornstein. 1985. "Clinical Understanding and Explaining: The Empathic Vantage Point." *Progress in Self Psychology* 1:43–61.

O'Shaughnessy, E. [1981] 1988. "W. R. Bion's Theory of Thinking and New Techniques in Child Analysis." In *Melanie Klein Today: Developments in Theory and Practice*, vol. 2, *Mainly Practice*, ed. E. Bott and E. B. Spillius. London: Routledge.

Price, M. 1993. "The Impact of Incest on Identity Formation in Women." *Journal of the American Academy of Psychoanalysis* 2 (12): 213–28.

Proust, M. 1981. *In Search of Lost Time*. 7 vols. New York: Random House.

Rachman, A. W. 1998. "Judicious Self-Disclosure by the Psychoanalyst." *International Forum of Psychoanalysis* 7 (4): 263–70.

Racker, H. 1957. "The Meaning and Uses of Countertransference." *Psychoanalytic Quarterly* 26:303–57.

Rankine, C. 2014. *Citizen: An American Lyric.* New York: Graywolf.

Reik, T. 1948. *Listening with the Third Ear.* New York: Grove.

Reineman, J. 2011. "Between the Imaginary and the Real: Photographic Portraits of Mourning and of Melancholia in Argentina." *International Journal of Psychoanalysis* 92:1241–61.

Renik, O. 1999. "Playing One's Cards Face-up in Analysis: An Approach to the Problem of Self-Disclosure." *Psychoanalytic Quarterly* 68 (4): 521–39.

Richards, A. 2014. "Freud's Jewish Identity and Psychoanalysis as a Science." *Journal of the American Psychoanalytic Association* 62 (6): 987–1003.

——. 2018. "Some Thoughts on Self-Disclosure." *Psychoanalytic Review* 105 (2): 137–56.

Richman, S. 2006. "Remembering to Forget to Remember: Response to Anna Ornstein." *Contemporary Psychoanalysis* 42 (4): 673–80.

Ringel, S. 2019. "Developmental Trauma and Unresolved Loss in the Adult Attachment Interview." *New Directions in Psychotherapy and Relational Psychoanalysis* 13:1–14.

Ringstrom, P. 2007. "Scenes That Write Themselves: Improvisational Moments in Relational Psychoanalysis." *Psychoanalytic Dialogues* 17:69–99.

Ritvo, S. 1971. "Late Adolescence: Developmental and Clinical Considerations." *Psychoanalytic Study of the Child* 26:241–63.

Rosenbaum, J. 2020. "Educational and Criminal Justice Outcomes 12 Years After School Suspension." *SAGE Journals* 52 (4): 515–47.

Rosenfeld, H. 1990. "Contributions to the Psychopathology of Psychotic States: The Importance of Projective Identification in the Ego Structure and Object Relations of the Psychotic Patient." In *Melanie Klein Today*, vol. 1: *Mainly Theory*, ed. E. Bott and E. B. Spillius. London: Routledge.

Ruddick, S. 2005. "What Do Mothers and Grandmothers Know and Want?" In *What Do Mothers Want? Developmental Perspectives,*

Clinical Challenges, ed. S. F. Brown, 69–86. Hillsdale, NJ: Analytic Press.

Russell, L. 2015. "Response to Andrew Balfour's 'Growing Old Together in Mind and Body.'" *Fort Da* 21 (2): 77–85.

Saad, L. 2020. Me and White Supremacy: Combat Racism, Change the World, and Become a Good Ancestor. Naperville, IL: Source.

Sacks, O. 2013. "Speak, Memory." *New York Review of Books*, February 21.

Sandler, J. 1987. "The Concept of Projective Identification." *Bulletin of the Anna Freud Centre* 10 (1): 33–49.

Sarton, M. 1978. "The Action of Therapy." In *Selected Poems of May Sarton*, ed. S. S. Hilsinger and L. Brynes, 197–202. New York: Norton.

Schacter, D. 1987. "Implicit Memory: History and Current Status." *Journal of Experiential Psychology* 13 (3): 501–18.

——. 1996. *Searching for Memory: The Brain, the Mind, and the Past*. New York: Basic Books.

Schafer, R. 1983. *The Analytic Attitude*. New York: Basic Books.

Schwaber, E. 1980. *Advances in Self-Psychology*. Ed. A. Goldberg. New York: International Universities Press.

——. 1981. "Empathy: A Mode of Analytic Listening." *Psychoanalytic Inquiry* 1 (3): 357–92.

——. 1992. "Countertransference: The Analyst's Retreat from the Patient's Vantage Point." *International Journal of Psycho-analysis* 73:349–61.

Searles, H. 1975. "The Patient as Therapist to his Analyst." In *Tactics and Techniques in Psychoanalytic Therapy*, vol. 2, ed. P. Giovacchini. New York: Jason Aronson.

Sherwin-White, S. 2014. "Melanie Klein's Thoughts on Brothers and Sisters." In *Sibling Matters: A Psychoanalytic, Developmental, and Systemic Approach*, ed. D. Hindle and S. Sherwin-White, 1–48. London: Karnac.

Shill, M. A. 2004. "Analytic Neutrality, Anonymity, Abstinence, and Elective Self-Disclosure." *Journal of the American Psychoanalytic Association* 52 (1): 151–87.

Siebold, C. 2011. "What Do Patients Want? Personal Disclosure and the Intersubjective Perspective." *Clinical Social Work Journal* 39 (2): 151–60.

Silverman, P. R., and J. W. Worden. 1993. "Children's Reactions to the Death of a Parent." In *Handbook of Bereavement: Theory, Research, and Intervention*, ed. M. S. Stroebe, W. Stroebe, and R. O. Hansson, 300–16. New York: Cambridge University Press.

Slavin, M., and D. Kriegman. 1998. "Why the Analyst Needs to Change: Toward a Theory of Conflict, Negotiation, and Mutual Influence in the Therapeutic Process." *Psychoanalytic Dialogues* 8:247–84.

Smilansky, S. 1987. *On Death: Helping Children Understand and Cope*. Bern: Peter Lang.

Smith, H. 2006. "Invisible Racism." *Psychoanalytic Quarterly* 75 (1): 3–19.

Spiegel, L. A. 1961. "Disorder and Consolidation in Adolescence." *Journal of the American Psychoanalytic Association* 9:406–16.

Spillius, E. B., and E. O'Shaughnessy. 2012. *When Theory Meets Practice: The Value and Limitations of the Concept of Projective Identification: The Fate of a Concept*. London: Routledge.

Spivak, A. 2014. "The Interpretive Process: The Power of 'Mere' Words." *Journal of the American Psychoanalytic Association* 62 (6): 1063–73.

Squire, L. R. 2009. "The Legacy of Patient HM for Neuroscience." *Neuron* 61 (1): 6–9.

Stern, D. 1985. *The Interpersonal World of the Infant*. New York: Basic Books.

——. 2004. *The Present Moment in Psychotherapy and Everyday Life*. New York: Norton.

Stern, D., and Process of Change Study Group. 1998. "The Process of Therapeutic Change Involving Implicit Knowledge: Some Implications of Developmental Observations for Adult Psychotherapy." *Infant Mental Health Journal* 19 (3): 300–8.

Stolorow, R. 2011. *Trauma and Human Existence*. New York: Analytic Press.

Stolorow, R., and G. Atwood. 1992. *Contexts of Being: The Intersubjective Foundations of Psychological Life*. Hillsdale, NJ: Analytic Press.

Stone, L. 1981. "Notes on the Non-Interpretive Elements in the Psychoanalytic Situation and Process." *Journal of the American Psychoanalytic Association* 29:89–118.

Suderman, H. 2020. "Radical Listening." *University of Washington Magazine*. https://magazine.washington.edu/feature/radical-listening/.

Sullivan, H. S. 1953. *The Interpersonal Theory of Psychiatry*. New York: Norton.

Sweezy, M. 2005. "Not Confidential: Therapist Considerations in Self-Disclosure." *Smith College Studies in Social Work* 75 (1): 81–91.

Tolpin, M. 2002. "Doing Psychoanalysis of Normal Development: Forward Edge Transferences." In *Progress in Self Psychology*, vol. 18, *Postmodern Self Psychology*, ed. A. Goldberg, 167–190. Hillsdale, NJ: Analytic Press.

Trenk-Hinterberger, S. 2014. "Experiences with Siblings in Early Childhood Specific Forms of Transference and Countertransference in Therapeutic Processes." In *Siblings*, ed. K. Skrzypek, B. Maciejewska-Sobczak, and Z. Stadnicka-Dmitriew, 179–91. London: Karnac.

Tulving, E. 1985. "Memory and Consciousness." *Canadian Psychology* 26:1–12.

U.S. Department of Education Office for Civil Rights. 2016. "Key Data Highlights on Equity and Opportunity Gaps in Our Nation's Public Schools." October 28, 2016.

Van der Kolk, B. A. 1996. *The Body Keeps the Score: Brain, Mind, and Body in the Healing of Trauma*. New York: Penguin.

Valent, P. 1998. "Resilience in Child Survivors of the Holocaust: Toward the Concept of Resilience." *Psychoanalytic Review* 85 (4): 517–35.

Wallin, D. 2007. *Attachment in Psychotherapy*. New York: Guilford.

Watts, T. 2014. "An Incestuous Development: A Study of Severe Psychopathology in a Fictive Adolescent from a Treatment." *Psychoanalytic Psychology* 31 (2): 262–75.

West, M. 2017. "Self-Disclosure, Trauma, and the Pressures on the Analyst." *Journal of Analytical Psychology* 62 (4): 585–601.

Wilkerson, I. 2020. *Caste: The Origins of Our Discontents*. New York: Random House.

Winer, R., and K. L. Malawista. 2017. *Who's Behind the Couch? The Heart and the Mind of the Psychoanalyst*. London: Karnac.

Winnicott, D. W. 1953. "Transitional Objects and Transitional Phenomena." *International Journal of Psychoanalysis* 34:89–97.

——. [1954] 1958. "Metaphysical and Clinical Aspects of Regression Within the Psychoanalytic Set-up." In *Collected Papers: Through Pediatrics to Psychoanalysis*. New York: Basic Books.

——. 1954–1955. "The Depressive Position in Normal Emotional Development." In *Collected Papers: Through Pediatrics to Psychoanalysis*, 89–100. New York: Basic Books.

——. [1958] 1965. "The Capacity to Be Alone." In *The Maturational Processes and the Facilitating Environment*, 29–36. New York: International Universities Press.

——. [1960] 1965. "Ego Distortion in Terms of True and False Self." In *The Maturational Processes and the Facilitating Environment*, 140–52. New York: International Universities Press.

——. [1963] 1965a. "The Development of the Capacity for Concern." In *The Maturational Processes and the Facilitating Environment*, 73–82. New York: International University Press.

——. [1963] 1965b. "From Dependence Towards Independence in the Development of the Individual." In *The Maturational Processes and the Facilitating Environment*, 83–92. New York: International Universities Press.

——. [1963] 1965c. "The Mentally Ill in Your Caseload." In *The Maturational Processes and the Facilitating Environment*, 217–29. New York: International University Press.

——. [1963] 1965d. "Dependence in Infant-Care, in Child-Care, and the Psycho-Analytic Setting." In *The Maturational Processes and the Facilitating Environment*, 250–60. New York: International University Press.

——. 1967. "The Location of Cultural Experience." *International Journal of Psychoanalysis* 48 (3): 213–31.

———. [1967] 1986. "Delinquency as a Sign of Hope." In *Home Is Where We Start From: Essays by a Psychoanalyst*, ed. C. Winnicott, R. Shepherd and M. Davies. New York: Norton.

Wolf, E. S. 1988. *Treating the Self*. New York: Guilford.

Wolfenstein, M. 1966. "How Is Mourning Possible? *Psychoanalytic Study of the Child* 21:93–123.

Wright, K. 1991. *Vision and Separations Between Mother and Baby*. Northvale, NJ: Jason Aronson.

INDEX

control by, 27, 33; COVID-19
and treatment of, 5, 180–82, 184;
denial by, 40; depression and,
26–27, 30–31; dreams by, 107,
109; fantasy by, 126;
responsiveness of, 39, 54, 111;
therapist change and change of,
133–34; therapist offices and
comfort of, 180–82; therapist
self-disclosure and, 136–37,
139–43
personal truths, 3, 184–85
phantasy, 42–44, 189n4
power: children wishing, 83;
reparation for omnipotent, 83;
whites and, 173
privilege. *See* white privilege
projective identification: causes of,
43; defense of, 43; guilt and, 44;
phantasy and, 42–44; racism as,
43; self and, 42–43; therapists
and, 41–42
Proust, Marcel, 13, 18–19
psychological defenses, 65–66
psychotherapy: definition, 1–2, 189n1

racism, 5; acknowledgment of, 171;
in caste system, 172–73; denial
on, 171–72; enactment and, 174;
as fantasy, 173–74; "hold another
in mind" and, 172; as projective
identification, 43; therapists and,
173–75; white privilege and,
169–75

Racker, H., 46
radical listening, 174
Rankine, Claudia, 172–73
remote connections, 176–82
reparation, 44, 83, 94, 100
resilience: by father, 5, 165–68;
Holocaust second generation and,
165–67; for human spirit, 180;
memory plasticity for, 3; for
mourning, 72; transitions and
challenges on, 4–5
responsiveness: as attuned, 122; of
children, 55, 91; as emotional
and human, 141–42; fear and,
63; as optimal, 113; of patient,
39, 54, 111; to sexual
exploitation, 159; of therapist,
35, 42, 46, 114, 174–75
Rich, Adrienne, 69, 80
Richman, Sophia, 166
Ringel, Shoshana, 159–60
Ringstrom, Philip, 140, 142
rivalry: envy or, 80, 84
roles: of parents, 99; shifting of, 100
Russell, Leslye, 102
Russo, Richard, 41

Sacks, Oliver, 3
Sandler, J., 43
Sarton, May, 99
Schafer, Roy, 112, 150–51
self: continuity of, 152; control of,
43; health and narrative of, 3–4;
knowledge of, 31; mind and,

GPSR Authorized Representative: Easy Access System Europe, Mustamäe tee
50, 10621 Tallinn, Estonia, gpsr.requests@easproject.com

www.ingramcontent.com/pod-product-compliance
Lightning Source LLC
Chambersburg PA
CBHW032134020426
42334CB00016B/1154